Marriage,
Divorce &
Nullity

Marriage, Divorce & Nullity

A Guide
to the Annulment Process
in the Catholic Church

Geoffrey Robinson

Foreword by Rev. Francis G. Morrisey, O.M.I.

Cover: Blaine Herrmann
Layout: Cynthia Roy

First published by Dove Communications, Blackburn, Victoria, Australia.

North American edition published 1987, 1993, 2000 by Novalis and
The Liturgical Press.

North American adaptations copyright ©1987 Novalis, Saint Paul
University, Ottawa, Canada.

Business Office:
Novalis
49 Front Street East, 2nd Floor
Toronto, Ontario, Canada
M5E 1B3

Phone: 1-800-387-7164 or (416) 363-3303
Fax: 1-800-204-4140 or (416) 363-9409
E-mail: novalis@interlog.com

The Liturgical Press
Collegeville, Minnesota
United States of America 56321

Printed in Canada

ISBN: Novalis 2-89507-099-7
       The Liturgical Press: 0-8146-1429-9

Canadian Cataloguing in Publication Data
Robinson, Geoffrey, 1937–
        Marriage, divorce & nullity: a guide to the annulment
process in the Catholic Church

Rev. ed.
Includes bibliographical references.
ISBN 2-89507-099-7

1. Marriage–Annulment (Canon law) 2. Marriage–
Religious aspects–Catholic Church. I. Title. II. Title:
Marriage, divorce and nullity.

BX2250.R62 2000   262.9'4   C00-900469-6

We acknowledge the financial support of the Government of Canada through the
Book Publishing Industry Development Program (BPIDP) for our publishing
activities.

Contents

Foreword 7

Preface 11

Chapter One
God's Plan for Marriage 15
    Creation 16
    Redemption 25

Chapter Two
Internal Forces in Marriage Breakdown 31
    Love and Reality 31
    Happiness Is a Serious Business 58

Chapter Three
External Forces in Marriage Breakdown 59
    The Nuclear Family 59
    Alienation 61
    The Rebellion of the 1960s 62
    Effects on Marriage 65
    Our Need for Each Other 68

Chapter Four
Learning to Live Again
After a Marriage Breakdown 71
    Bereavement 71

Learning to Live Again 73
Children 77
Learning Through
Separation and Divorce............................ 79
Remarriage.. 80

Chapter Five
As Long as We Both Shall Live 83
The Teaching of Jesus 83
Beliefs and Laws 86
The Greater Good?............................... 87
Guilt and Innocence 89
Separation, Divorce, Remarriage.......... 90

Chapter Six
Weddings that Are Not Marriages.............. 93
Every Wedding Is Public 93
Decrees of Nullity 95
Catholic Objections 96
Church Laws on Marriage..................... 97
Impediments....................................... 98
Form.. 100
Consent.. 101

Chapter Seven
Approaching a Tribunal 105
Questions Asked by Applicants 106
Stages of the Procedure 122

Footnotes 123

Foreword

For centuries the Catholic Church has proclaimed the indissolubility of marriage. In spite of strong opposition from many circles, it has steadfastly taught that we must not separate what God has joined together. Well-known figures, such as St. Thomas More, even gave their lives for this principle and are revered throughout the world today for their fidelity to a basic understanding of marriage.

On the other hand, the Church has also recognized that there are exceptions to the principle when stated in its broadest terms. St. Paul, in his first letter to the Corinthians (7:13), provided for certain situations—now known as the Pauline Privilege—when a marriage was entered into between two non-baptized persons. If one of the parties was subsequently baptized and could no longer live in peace because the other party gave offence to the Creator, then a new marriage was authorized. It was also recognized that marriages could not take place within prohibited degrees of relationships (see 1 Corinthians 5:11), when there was a total lack of freedom, when a person was a eunuch (see Matthew 19:12), and so forth.

With the passage of time the Church became aware of other circumstances that prevented a marriage from coming into existence. The list of impediments was extended to cover such areas as lack of age, absence of baptism, abduction, and so forth. Likewise, it became evident that some people were consenting to a union on their own terms, excluding such essential elements as fidelity, indissolubility, or openness to children. Church courts began to declare that such unions were not true marriages and these were consequently declared null.

In the twentieth century two events marked in a particular way the Church's understanding of marriage nullity. One was Pius XII's call (October 3, 1941) for a prudent use of the new discoveries of the behavioral sciences, in particular psychology and psychiatry, in examining unfortunate situations of marriage breakdown. It became evident that in some cases people were not unwilling to enter into marriage but rather were incapable of doing so—their thought processes were severely impaired, their judgment was seriously affected, they were unable to assume the essential obligations of marriage. With the help of the behavioral sciences, it became somewhat easier to understand not only why marriages failed but also why some people were not eligible to enter into such unions.

The second major event was the renewed teaching on the sacrament of marriage proposed by the Second Vatican Council in the pastoral constitution *Gaudium et spes*. With a particular emphasis placed on the conjugal community of life and love, and with new insights into the importance of the well-being of the spouses themselves being proclaimed officially, people—canon lawyers in particular—began to look at various situations of marriage breakdown to see whether these unions met the Church's requirements for a truly sacramental marriage.

In the late 1960s, shortly after the Council, canon law societies around the world began to address this delicate question, taking into account particular circumstances of geography and culture. A number of these societies—such as those of Australia and New Zealand, Canada, Great Britain and Ireland, the United States of America—began to share the results of their findings and consolidate the data that was subsequently incorporated into the revised code of Canon Law promulgated by Pope John Paul II in 1983.

One of those who was deeply involved in such research was Bishop Geoffrey Robinson, who at the time was Chief Justice of the Tribunal of the Archdiocese of Sydney, Australia, and subsequently became president of the Canon Law Society of Australia and New Zealand. In 1984 he was ordained a bishop and, while still continuing to work in the marriage tribunal, has assumed new responsibilities in the Church.

It is the result of his years of study, prayer, and reflection that we find brought together in this publication, which has been slightly adapted for North American readership. Few people would have been better qualified for this task. We find expressed in these pages not only an intense desire to remain faithful to the Gospel teachings but also a deep concern for couples who have faced tragic situations in their wedded life.

It is our hope that this work will help clarify a number of issues for Catholics and also provide hope and comfort for some people who otherwise might not have been able to avail themselves of the Church's pastoral concern for them.

Francis G. Morrisey, O.M.I.
Faculty of Canon Law
Saint Paul University
Ottawa, Canada

Preface

The main purpose of this book is to try to reach out to Catholics whose marriage has broken down. I would like to show them that the Church has not cut them off or forgotten their existence. It is hoped that an explanation of Catholic principles will help them feel accepted in and at peace with the Church. I would like to show them how the Church may possibly help them to resolve some of their problems through a decree of nullity, to answer some of the most common questions asked, and to resolve the fears felt about decrees of nullity.

As I worked on the book, however, it became clear to me that I could not do this without attempting to reassure the many married Catholics who fear that decrees of nullity are destroying Catholic teaching and threatening their own marriages by denying the ideals of marriage that the Church has always held. Unless the whole community understands, it will continue to be difficult to help divorced Catholics. Thus this book is addressed to all Catholics.

I therefore felt it was necessary to say something not just about divorce and nullity, but about marriage itself. I had to expound the ideal of marriage as seen through the eyes of Christian faith, marriage as God created it and means it to be. I had to encourage couples to seek this high ideal of marriage with all their strength. This has been the aim of Chapter One.

Ideals cannot be achieved unless they have a firm basis in reality, so Chapter Two deals with the human reality of marriage. It asks many of the ordinary, down-to-earth questions that must be faced if a marriage is to have a firm basis. It also shows how marriages can break down from within.

Chapter Three shows how external forces can break down marriages. It speaks of some of the changes at work in Western society that cause problems in marriages. Chapter Four is an attempt to explain to the whole community some of the special difficulties that divorced persons face.

In Chapter Five I have presented the Church's teaching that a true marriage lasts until death. In Chapter Six I have tried to show that throughout history a wedding ceremony has not always and automatically produced a marriage. In Chapter Seven I have sought to answer the most frequent questions and the most common fears of people who are thinking of approaching a Church tribunal to seek a decree of nullity.

Church tribunals have always been strongly criticized by two different groups of people. The first group consists of Catholics who believe that there should be no decrees of nullity at all, that a person is married until death and there can be no exceptions. The second group consists of Catholics who believe that tribunals are a medieval relic in a church that should accept civil divorce as ending a marriage. For diametrically opposed reasons, therefore, both sides believe that tribunals should not exist. The issue arouses strong emotions in both groups.

Many people will consider me foolhardy for jumping into such a stormy sea. I do so because standing on the shore helps no one. The Church seeks to hold to the principles it believes came from Jesus Christ himself, and at the same time give whatever help it can within these principles to troubled people.

The controversy surrounding the granting of decrees of nullity has given rise to popular folklore about tribunals that bears little resemblance to reality. Some of the ideas in this book may, therefore, be new and unfamiliar to readers. I only ask readers to approach them with an open mind. It is difficult to speak to two opposing groups simultaneously, while not forgetting those who stand in the middle. The attempt must be made so that people who are in need can be helped. This book may seem to cover many subjects, but I believe that all of them are essential to the understanding of the question of marriage and nullity within the Catholic Church.

Geoffrey Robinson
Sydney, Australia

Chapter One

God's Plan for Marriage

$\mathcal{I}$n living their day-to-day lives and in meeting the difficulties that face them, married couples receive help from friends and neighbours and from various professional people and agencies, such as schools, doctors and counsellors.

Catholics are among these friends, neighbours and professional people, but is the help they give different in any way from that given by other people? In other words, is there any specifically Catholic assistance that can be offered to married couples?

Many people would answer this question by saying that the Church has its own agencies, such as schools and counsellors. They will point to the assistance that the parish community can give, and speak of particular Catholic friends and neighbours.

The answer must, however, be more basic than this. It must be found in our understanding of marriage as seen through the eyes of Christian faith, in our Catholic understanding of God's plan for marriage. Only if this is present can we begin to talk of a specifically Catholic contribution from friends, schools or any other agency. If Catholics are not working from such a basis, then they have nothing to offer that others cannot provide equally well. Thus it is with a personal attempt at such an understanding or vision of marriage that this book must begin.

I shall do this under the two headings of creation and redemption. *Creation* will tell us something of what God means marriage to be for all people of all times, irrespective of race, colour or creed. *Redemption* will tell us what God means marriage to be for Christian people.

Creation

In answering the question about divorce, Jesus said, "Have you not read that the creator from the beginning made them male and female..." (Matthew 19:3-6). He referred his hearers back to the story of the creation, indicating that that was the place to begin any study of marriage, for that would tell us God's original plan for marriage, what God meant it to be for all people of all times.

1. The Bible Account

About a thousand years before Christ, a writer looked carefully at the people of the time and at the way they related to God and to one another. Under the guidance of divine inspiration, the writer discerned in these people God's original plan for the human race and presented this plan in the second chapter of the Book of Genesis. It is not an eyewitness account of the creation, but a story like one of the parables that Jesus used so often. As in the gospel parables, here too we have to go behind the story told, and then we find many inspired truths about ourselves and our relationship with God and with one another.

The story says that "God fashioned man of dust from the soil. Then he breathed into his nostrils a breath of life, and thus man became a living being" (2:7). In this opening to the story, God is telling us that we are made of earthly, material elements but that God has breathed into these elements the divine spirit of life. Body and soul are not separate; they make one person, so that we are spirit-made-flesh, spirit incarnate.[1]

God's act of creation is an act of love, and every act of love is a call for a return of love. Love is, therefore, our first and fundamental vocation.[2] We want to return God's love, to reach out and be fully united, but spirit is united with body and this prevents it from being fully united with God. Thus we feel a restlessness and dissatisfaction. We are always reaching out for something higher. We cannot ever be totally content.

So, in the parable, God says, "It is not good that the man should be alone. I will make him a helpmate" (2:18). The English word "helpmate" may seem to imply an inferior being, a helper of some lower order, but the Hebrew word it is translating, *ezer,* is used many times for God as our mighty helper, and so certainly implies nothing inferior or secondary.

"So from the soil God fashioned all the wild beasts and all the birds of heaven. These he brought to the man to see what he would call them" (2:19). For the Hebrews, to give something a name meant two things—that they had power over the thing to be named and that they understood its nature fully. In the parable these two conditions are fulfilled, so "The man gave names to all cattle, all the birds of heaven and all the wild beasts" (2:20).

We like animals and find companionship in them. However, they are "from the soil," so they cannot satisfy our deeper longings. We seek the divine from whence the spirit of life came, and it cannot be found here. "No helpmate suitable for man was found for him" (2:20).

"So God made the man fall into a deep sleep. And while he slept, he took one of his ribs and enclosed it in flesh. God built the rib he had taken from the man into a woman, and brought her to the man" (2:21-22). The idea of a rib may have been used because in a common language of the time (Sumerian) the word *ti* means both rib and life. Certainly the idea is that it is the life or spirit of the man that becomes the woman. On seeing her, the man can only exclaim, "This at last is bone from my bones, and flesh from my flesh! This is to be called woman, for this was taken from man" (2:23).

The Hebrew word for man used here is *ish*. The word used for woman is *ishsha*—the same word, but with a feminine ending. This is something we are not familiar with in English, but it is common in other languages. For example, in Russia, the wife of Mr. Romanov is not called Mrs. Romanov but Mrs. Romanova, the same name but with a feminine ending. If an Italian man wishes to say that he is happy, he says that he is *contento*, while a woman would say that she is *contenta*. Once again these are not two different words, but the same word with masculine and feminine endings. This is what happens in the account of creation. The man says, "This is to be called *ishsha* for this was taken from *ish*."

There is an important truth behind this. It means that the man cannot name the woman, he can only call her by his own name with a feminine ending. He cannot name her because the two conditions for giving a name are not fulfilled. Firstly, the man has no power over her, as he has over the animals, for it is his own life or spirit that has become the woman. Secondly, his knowledge cannot penetrate to her being, for the spirit of life that came from God is within her and he can never fully penetrate this.

Precisely because she is his equal, and only for this reason, he finds satisfaction and fulfillment in her. The animals he could name, and so they do not satisfy him; the woman he cannot name, and so he does find satisfaction in her. It is not as great as the total satisfaction he will find only in God, whose name the Hebrew was not even to say out loud, but it is a satisfaction that takes away much of the loneliness and restlessness he felt before. Because she has the same divine spirit of life, he can find something of the divine in her and she in him. True love between them is an intuitive glimpse of the divine in each other.

The union of man and woman is thus presented as the first and most fulfilling human relationship. "This is why a man leaves his father and mother and joins himself to his wife, and they become one body" (2:24). Other relationships, even important ones such as those with parents, are put into second place so that this one may be complete.

Man and woman do not meet as two spirits, but as two human beings, spirits incarnate. Their sexuality is part of their being and of their ability to relate. "Now both of them were naked, the man and his wife, but they felt no shame in front of each other" (2:25).[3]

A few hundred years later a second account of creation was written, this time in the form of a parable of the seven days of creation. Though later in time, it was placed as the first chapter of Genesis, before the older account. It takes up the same ideas when it says that humankind was created in the image and likeness of God (1:26).

This image and likeness to God is not a physical, photographic image. It does not mean that physically we look like God, but expresses a deep spiritual reality. It means that we alone have received the divine spirit of life, we alone long for the infinite, we alone share in the divine life in a special way.

For most human beings, it is in their relationships with other persons that they find their deepest and most constant satisfaction. Marriage offers to two persons the opportunity to know and love each other at a depth that nothing else on earth can quite offer. Because God is within the other, marriage may be called a voyage of discovery of the infinite.

Being married does not achieve this state automatically. A couple can fail to learn how to love, and they can be prevented from seeing the divine in each other. This goal can never be achieved in one moment. Marriage can do no more than offer the opportunity, but it does this better than any other relationship on earth.

The word "enthusiasm" comes from two Greek words, *en* (within) and *theos* (god), and so means the "god-within." When a person is really enthusiastic about something, it seems as though there is a god-within inspiring that person. The married couple can face each other with the enthusiasm of love as they embark on the voyage of discovery of God within each other. No matter how long they live, there will always be more to discover, for the infinite is reflected there.

God blesses the first married couple and says to them, "Be fruitful, multiply, fill the earth and conquer it. Be masters of the fish of the sea, the birds of heaven and all living animals on the earth" (1:28). It is man and woman together who are given this blessing and responsibility. "God saw all he had made, and indeed it was very good" (1:31).

2. Three Qualities of Marriage

From these two accounts of creation we can deduce three particular qualities that God means each marriage to have: marriage is meant to be between one man and one woman; to last their entire lives; and to produce new life.

(a) One man and one woman. "I am the Lord your God...You shall have no gods except me" (Exodus 20:1-3). There is only one God, and it is the same God who is present in each human person. Whether we seek God in one person or many, it is the same God whom we are seeking.

God, however, respects our individuality. God does not take over our whole personalities in such a way that it would not matter whom one married because one would not be loving that person in himself/herself, but only God-within. There is only one God, but God has many images. It is the incarnate reality of a particular image of God with whom a person falls in love. Men and women strive for the infinite, but they belong to this earth, so it is a genuine human love they feel for a fellow human being. It is simultaneously human and divine love they seek in each other.

Everyone should seek to love every single image of God, every person on the face of the earth, but if marriage is to achieve the purpose of helping a couple to find and love God in their love for each other, then it must be a long process of discovery, which can be achieved only by total commitment to one person. God exists in the depths of our being, and there are no easy shortcuts in this journey. The experience must be a slow, deep and lasting one.

This total love for another makes a person vulnerable, open to be hurt by the other. Thus every act of infidelity is an injury to the other, who is building his or her whole life on trusting another and on finding both human and divine love in that other. Promiscuity is the failure to find real satisfaction in anything beyond that which can be seen and touched. It is the failure to find God within others. The giving of one's body to another is always something of a lie, unless it is part of the total giving of all of oneself forever. Pre-marital sex and adultery are wrong because, in varying degrees, they contain this lie.[4]

(b) For their entire lives: love and commitment.[5] A couple who live together without marriage may feel fully committed to each other. They may bear and raise

children. They may be convinced that their union is more authentic precisely because there are no legal and social bonds constraining them. To them it may be more genuine because it depends entirely on their willing it to continue.

However, without marriage they are falling short of total commitment. Love always aspires to permanence. To love another totally, but only for a time, is a contradiction in terms. Thus the couple who live together without marriage face a dilemma. If from the very beginning each understands that he or she is free to leave at any time, then they are not willing the good of the other totally, for there are limits and reservations to their love. If their love is to be complete, then each has to say to himself or herself: I am not free to leave without denying the love I gave, without being untrue to myself.

Many are afraid of this total love. They fear that things may go wrong in the relationship, and they do not want to be hurt if this happens. So their love is conditional: if we still love each other.... They seek to lighten the load of obligations by doing away with the legal and social bonds, but they cannot do this without denying to each other the security of total love. This is a fear of love. It is also a denial of love, because it places limits. There cannot be total love where there are limits. It is not an unreserved giving, for there is the conscious or unconscious realization that circumstances may arise in which they will want to separate.

For many people, marriage is entered into with the same thoughts and feelings. The couple may hope and believe that their marriage will last forever, and they may intend to work for this, but the reservation is there. This reservation can easily become a self-fulfilling prophecy: because they expect problems to arise, problems do arise. One of the best ways to assist young couples is, therefore, to help them to overcome their fear of total commitment and of the vulnerability that comes with it. Such a commitment can help to ensure that problems do not arise by default—in other words, by doing nothing about them.

A faith understanding of marriage would add that if a person has any reservations at all on love, then that person is much less likely to find God in the other.

As persons, we are shaped by our decisions and the way we stand by them. They enter into our being and make us the persons we are. A total commitment in marriage is the most important decision that most people will ever make. Through it, two people give to each other and to themselves an identity and a name. More than almost anything else, the nature of the commitment they give in marriage both expresses and shapes the persons they are.

Because it matters what a person does, it matters also what that person has done in the past. The significance of past actions can be ignored only at the cost of admitting that nothing matters at all. If a person thoughtlessly abandons one marriage and enters another, how can that person now promise "for better, for worse, till death do us part," if this promise has already been made to someone else? The commitment is what makes the marriage. It cannot be weakened without compromising the whole relationship.

(c) To produce new life. Just as God's love was fruitful in the creation of humankind, so this deepest human union of man and woman is meant to be fruitful. With God they co-create another image of God with the same presence of the infinite. It is at the moment of the birth of their first child that a couple are usually most aware of the presence of the infinite. There is a sense of wonder as they hold their first baby in their arms, an awareness

that there is something there beyond their own power to create. While it is more intense at that moment, it is a permanent reality of their marriage, even when it seems obscured. It can give them a sense of reverence for each other and for their children—not the reverence that causes fear or prevents action, but the sense of being in the presence of something of great dignity and lasting value.

The obligation to "be fruitful and multiply" (Genesis 1:28) is given to the human race as a whole. It does not mean that each couple is bound to have as many children as possible, so the concept of responsible parenthood is fully in accord with God's original plan. This means that the couple should recognize fully their duties towards God, towards themselves, towards their family and towards society, in a correct scale of values.

3. Sin

In chapter three of Genesis, sin enters the picture in the account of the Fall and seriously affects the relationships between man and woman (3:16), between them and nature (3:17-19) and between them and God (3:23). All the evil things that are present in the male–female relationship are presented as the result of sin. Polygamy, use of the other as an object rather than as a person, lust without love, violence and sadism, domination and subservience—all of those things are presented as a fall from the way God meant things to be for our happiness and advancement.

The words "your yearning shall be for your husband, yet he will lord it over you" (3:16) are not a divine punishment of the female and a justification for male domination. They express the results of the Fall from the way God created man and woman and meant them to relate.

"Then the eyes of both of them were opened and they realized that they were naked" (3:7). They awoke to sin and to all the turmoil that this introduced into their lives, but in another sense their eyes were closed and they lost sight of the divine in each other. It was now fallen man and fallen woman and, therefore, fallen marriage that they had to contend with. The following chapters and books of the Bible give us many examples of marriages that were far from the creation.

Though Christ has now redeemed the world, we too are still fallen man and fallen woman, damaged in our relationships and struggling to regain the creation. In relation to marriage, this struggle to regain the original plan of creation was the major radical call that Christ made: "Have you not read that the creator from the beginning made them male and female..." (Matthew 19:4).

Redemption

After creation, the other central idea of scripture is that of redemption. In the Old Testament it is prepared for by God's love for the people of the covenant. In seeking to express that love, the prophets turned frequently to the image of marriage.[6] Marriage became, as it were, a mirror in which something of God's love was seen as reflected. In this process, marriage was in its turn illuminated by the covenant: if husband and wife loved each other as God loved, then they would indeed be returning to the creation. Though it is present in the Old Testament, we shall look at it in its fullness in Christ.

1. The New Commandment

In John 13:34 Jesus says, "I give you a new commandment: love one another...." At first sight there is nothing new about this commandment. In expressing the twin commandments of love of God and love of neighbour,

Jesus is doing nothing more than quoting Deuteronomy 6:4-5 and Leviticus 19:18. Most people of his time were already very familiar with these commandments as the greatest of them all. The newness of the commandments is in the words immediately following: "just as I have loved you, you also must love one another." In Jesus the love of God is being shown more fully and more intensely than ever before. To love as Jesus loved was new, for no one had ever shown such love before.

For Christians the covenant between God and the chosen people has become the covenant between Christ and the Church. It is the same divine love in both covenants, but it is now being shown more intensely. The words and deeds of Christ, therefore, give us a whole new understanding of what husband and wife can hope to find in each other and of the way in which they ought to act towards each other.

The words quoted were spoken by Christ at the Last Supper, when the thought of the cross filled his mind. On the cross he was rejected and abandoned. He was nailed to the wood, so that even physically he could not go out to make a final plea to the people for a reconciliation. He could only love them in his solitude with a greater love than ever. This is love taken to a divine degree.

Thus it is an enormous thing when husbands are told to love their wives "as Christ loved the Church and sacrificed himself for her" (Ephesians 5:25). To the creation idea of fidelity there is added the covenant idea of love and fidelity of Jesus. In loving as Christ loved, man and woman will come to the full realization of God's plan of creation.

2. The Trinity

In the language of symbol we may speak of God as a family.[7] The essence of the Trinity is that the Persons are united yet distinct: three in one. Husband and wife are also united yet distinct: two in one. Like God they too give new life. With their child they become three in one. To the creation idea of finding God in the other, Christian revelation adds the idea of finding the creative, innermost life of God in their family. A family is a fuller image of God than an individual.

Obviously, there can be no simple identification of husband with Father, wife with Son and child with Spirit. We are speaking analogy and symbol, which cannot be pushed too far. It is aspects of God rather than definite Persons that are reflected.

All human beings in their different ways reflect something of God. No human being can reflect God fully. Men often reflect certain aspects of God more strongly, women often bring out more clearly certain other aspects. Naturally, we cannot neatly categorize aspects of God as masculine or feminine. Strength does not belong to men alone, gentleness and compassion are not attributes of women alone. What is true is that man, woman and child together will reflect God more fully than any one of them could do alone. God is neither male nor female; God is God.

3. Sacrament

The Church sees marriage between two Christians as a sacrament. Marriage is both a covenant between the couple and a covenant between the two of them and God. The call to married life is, in the true sense of the word, a vocation, a calling from God. However, it is not enough for God to call the couple to this covenant and invite them to model it on the covenant between Christ and the Church. It is also necessary that God offer them the promise of divine grace that will sustain the covenant and make the idea of regaining the creation a real possibility. The union between the couple must itself become the sacred sign or sacrament of this promise of divine grace.

There are two ways in which marriage is different from any of the other six sacraments. It is the only sacrament in which the persons involved are themselves the "matter" of the sacrament. By matter I mean the material substance that is used in celebrating the sacrament (e.g., water in baptism, oil in confirmation or the anointing of the sick). The matter of a sacrament always symbolizes the spiritual reality and is said to be a "visible sign of invisible grace": e.g., water physically cleans, refreshes and purifies, just as baptism does these things spiritually. In the same way oil physically strengthens, soothes and heals, just as confirmation and anointing do this spiritually. In marriage the union of the couple is itself the symbol of God's action in helping their union to be complete. There is no need of any other symbol external to themselves.

The second difference follows from this. In all other sacraments the bishop or priest is the normal minister; in marriage he is not. The priest has an important role as the official witness at the wedding, representing the entire community, but it is the husband who is the minister of the sacrament to his wife and the wife who is the minister of the sacrament to her husband. Furthermore, when a priest baptizes a baby or confers any other sacrament, he may or may not see that person again, but in marriage there is a continuing close relationship between minister and recipient that is unlike any other sacrament. While the sacrament is received at one moment, the grace of the sacrament continues to be administered and received throughout the couple's lives. Thus their gift of themselves to each other is a gift of grace.

Grace is God at work within us with a power similar to the inspiration of the artist, the enthusiasm of the idealist, the devotion of the lover. Such people seem to work with an inner power that makes them not less but more free, not less but more themselves, capable of achievements beyond their normal personalities, and yet achievements that are wholly their own. In marriage, the couple are meant to mediate this grace to each other.

Because the couple are still fallen humanity, this mediation of grace is essential. Their marriage is filled with the difficulties of ordinary, limited and sinful humanity struggling to regain the creation. There is thus a constant need to experience conversion of heart. Because of their limitations and sinfulness, their married love involves that death to self that makes it truly Christian. The forgiveness received from the other is an experience of Christ's forgiveness and grace mediated through the other.

The divinely inspired writers introduced marriage into the very first pages of the Bible when presenting God's original plan for the world. This alone should tell us of its importance.

The New Testament begins with the birth of Jesus in a human family. After spending most of his life with that family, Jesus began his public ministry, at the invitation of his mother, with a miracle at Cana in which he abundantly blessed the ordinary joys of a wedding day by turning water into wine. He ended his public life by returning to his concern for family with these words:

"Woman, this is your son... This is your mother." The very next words of St. John's Gospel are: "After this, Jesus knew that everything had now been completed..." (John 19:26-28).

Jesus came on earth to change human society in all places and all times. To accomplish this, he knew that the place to begin and the place to end was the family. If he is a guest and witness at each wedding, part of the covenant throughout each marriage, then his mission is being achieved.

Some years ago I took communion to a very elderly lady in the parish. Her equally elderly husband met me at the door and led me to her room. As we walked in, all I could see in the bed was a very elderly person asleep with her mouth open, but her husband stopped as we entered, looked at her for a few moments and said softly, "Oh, Father, isn't she beautiful." That couple had very nearly regained the creation.

Chapter Two

Internal Forces in Marriage Breakdown

*T*he ideal just presented is not always realized. People who enter marriage with high hopes of the happiness it will bring may one day find themselves in a divorce court. Each breakdown has its own unique and private history behind it, and there are many different factors that can lead to it. In this chapter I shall consider those that come from within the marriage itself.

Love and Reality

Being in love makes a young couple feel so good that it overwhelms everything else in their lives. It is so wonderful that the young couple feel that love must overcome all problems. All difficulties of identity, insecurity, self-esteem and acceptance seem to disappear. The young couple can feel that people who have been divorced cannot possibly have loved as they now love. They may give lip service to the idea that there is more to the story than this, but frequently they don't really believe it. They find it hard to grasp the idea that older people, such as their parents, were ever really young and in love as they now are.

No one would wish to crush young love or take away its beauty. God created it, and it has a most important part to play in the success of marriage. In the first chapter I said that it is an intuitive glimpse of the divine in the other. We must also accept the illusions that go with it. I therefore believe that the best way of communicating with such couples is to accept the fact of their love, but then try to lead them to see what this love asks of them.

On the one hand, I believe that most young couples, if left to themselves, do not discuss the serious issues involved in marriage and, indeed, would not be able to identify many of the issues. On the other hand, I have found that, if invited and helped to do so, most young couples are very willing to enter into such discussions. I find most of them extremely honest, though there can be resistance if the discussions begin to lead them towards conclusions they do not wish to reach.

Love is to will the good of another person, making one ready to do everything for that person. The more one knows of the needs, hopes, problems, strengths and weaknesses of that other, the better one can achieve his or her good. Love therefore demands that the couple try to answer the questions connected with this.

I shall try to list some of the more important topics. While I have directly had in mind a couple preparing for marriage for the first time, I have tried to make the questions relevant also to a couple who are already married and, indeed, to a person entering a second marriage.

Through these questions I hope to show some of the ways in which a marriage can break down from within. They express something of the human reality that must serve as a basis if the ideal of the first chapter is to be attained.

1. Interests and Activities

No one person can hope to meet all the needs of another person. Each party to a marriage will therefore need other friends and interests. There must be a balance between these interests and the needs of the marriage. This means that to a large extent it is desirable that the friends and interests be held in common, though room must be left for some individual interests not held by the other. As well as complementing each other by common tastes and interests, it is good that the couple also challenge each other to new ideas and interests. At the beginning of the marriage, the primary need will be to make the transition from the single to married life, so there will need to be an emphasis on common friends, interests and activities.

 Some Questions for the Couple:

Am I comfortable with my partner's friends?

Is my partner comfortable with mine?

Does each of us have true friends?

If not, what is the reason for this and is it saying something serious about one or both of us?

What are my partner's hobbies and interests? Can I share them?

What are my hobbies and interests? Can my partner share them?

Are these interests limited to (for example) television and, if so, what is this saying about us?

Whatever seeming discussion takes place, do we in fact always end up going to places and following the interests chosen by only one of us?

Am I prepared to put up with this pattern for the rest of my life?

Is my partner too busy with work to have time to spend with me?

Does my partner talk about his/her job and allow me to take an interest in it?

Do I respond and take an interest?

Am I willing to do the same concerning my own job?

Can we live with our choice of different political parties?

How would my partner react if I voted for a different party?

Do my partner's hobbies cost more money than we can afford?

If so, have we discussed this, and what is the outcome?

2. Roles in Marriage

Some people who are marrying today were raised in families where men's and women's roles were traditional: the man earned a living to support the family and the woman did most of the child-rearing and managing of the home. There have been many changes in our understanding of male and female roles in our world, and couples today can find themselves facing many questions concerning who does what in the marriage. Couples who claim to want to share the various tasks and roles equally need to be clear about the implications of equality in their daily lives, so that they accept the practice of equality as well as the theory. Statistically, marriages are more tranquil when husband and wife keep to more traditional roles, because the patterns are more familiar and require less thought and possibly dangerous experimentation. This is not an argument for making no changes, but it is wise to be aware of the pitfalls. Even when an apparently clear agreement is reached, one or other partner can return to more familiar patterns.

In practice, most people follow the patterns of their parents' marriage. They do this even when they are rebelling against the parents' model of marriage, for it is the pattern they are most familiar with. There is nothing wrong with this provided the parents' pattern was a reasonably satisfactory one for both father and mother, and provided the pattern was the same in the marriages of both sets of parents of the young couple. It will not work if the pattern did not work for the parents, or if the two patterns were quite different, e.g., if the man's father was dominant in his family, while the woman's mother was dominant in her family. It needs little imagination to see what will happen in such a case if the young couple attempt to follow the patterns each learned at home.

? *Some Questions for the Couple:*

What were the roles in my parents' marriage?

What were the roles in the marriage of my partner's parents?

Did these roles work for them? Did any one person have to pay a serious price for the roles adopted?

In what ways were the roles in the two families different?

If we are going to follow the patterns of our parents, how will the differences in patterns need to be adjusted?

If we are not going to follow the patterns of our parents, what patterns do we wish to follow?

Are we both capable of these new patterns?

Is my partner truly convinced concerning the new patterns and so won't complain too often about them?

Will either of us frequently fall back into more familiar roles, especially should some upset or difficulty occur?

What will be my reaction if my partner starts reverting to a traditional role?

How fixed and immovable are my partner's attitudes towards roles?

Is there anything at all that I consider to be my partner's sole responsibility, not mine?

Is there anything my partner considers to be my responsibility alone?

Do we have the same attitudes to working wives? to work within the home? to work on the outside of the house and in the garden? to the care of children?

In what ways is male chauvinism present in the husband?

Does the wife truly believe herself to be his equal?

What difficulties does she have in asserting this?

Does the husband give practical as well as intellectual assent to the idea that the wife is his equal?

3. Choice of Partner

It has been said that people don't change, they only become more so! This is not quite true, but the changes that may occur within people occur only along lines that are consistent with their personalities and their beliefs. The general traits of an individual's personality will probably remain the same throughout his or her life. It is wiser to assume that the person one marries will not change. Certainly it is unwise to assume that the particular changes one partner wishes for will be the ones that will occur in the other. If both partners agree that change is desirable, then this should occur prior to marriage. To pressure a partner after marriage is likely to elicit this response: "I am the person I am. You knew what I was like when you married me."

? *Some Questions for the Couple:*

Am I disturbed by my partner's temper? use of tobacco, alcohol, other drugs? gambling? spending of money? moodiness and depressions? sense of humour?

Am I uncomfortable with my partner's behaviour at social functions? with my friends? at my home? with my partner's own friends or own family?

Am I often displeased with my partner's dress and appearance?

Am I annoyed by certain mannerisms?

Am I bothered by the way my partner shows affection to me in public? does not show affection?

Do I fear that my partner might have homosexual tendencies?

Do I trust my partner with members of my own sex?

Is my partner too dependent on parents? on the opinion of friends?

Am I worried by my partner's prejudices against certain individuals or groups?

Do I have any worries about the mental health of my partner?

Is my partner generally satisfied with life?

Does my partner frequently change jobs?

Is my partner frequently out of a job when employment is available?

Am I worried whether my partner will settle to married life?

Am I satisfied with the way my partner handles personal problems? problems that occur between the two of us?

4. Personal Readiness for Marriage

Many people consider the choice of a good partner to be the entire secret to the success of marriage. It is of course of great importance, but it is only half the secret. The other half is whether you are ready for marriage yourself. If you bring difficulties to the marriage, they will cause problems. A good partner may be more tolerant, but there will still be problems. Marriage will magnify personal problems rather than solve them. Time heals wounds, but does not of itself solve problems. It is much better if you seek to solve any personal problems before you come to marriage. If professional assistance is needed, it is better to seek it now.

? *Some Questions for the Couple:*

All of the questions asked in the previous section, "Choice of Partner," concerning your partner need to be applied to yourself as well. They are different ways of asking whether you are ready for marriage. To them one could add:

In what ways do I need to change now before I enter marriage?

Would professional assistance be of benefit to me in resolving personal problems that might otherwise cause difficulties in the marriage?

5. Religion

Not many young couples see religion as an important question in their preparation for marriage. If invited to think about it they see it largely in terms of whether one or both of them will go to church on Sundays, and feel they can easily live with whatever answer the partner gives. Religion will, however, affect their marriage in many more ways than this. It is in religious faith, or in its absence, that the highest goals of marriage are found and that a person finds the basis of his or her identity and dignity as an individual. Difference in religion is also one of the most common causes of crossed lines of communication in marriage. For example, a husband is coming home drunk most evenings, so his wife refuses to make love. Rather than confront the real issue between them (what is causing him to drink), he can put the blame onto religion: "It's all your Catholic hang-ups about sex."

Or the opposite can happen: a non-Catholic wife can fear that the Catholic upbringing of the children will somehow take the children away from her. This is a threatening idea, too threatening to discuss; so she complains about something only marginally related to what is really worrying her, e.g., finances. In this case it is religion that the couple ought to be discussing, but the message is not getting through and the husband is bewildered. Religion touches deep subjects, which explains why it is so often used in this way. Even if a couple were to agree that religion was of no importance to either of them, they would still be giving personal answers to questions concerning their deepest values in life, and these answers will come to the surface in a thousand different ways.

? Some Questions for the Couple:

Who am I? Where do I come from? Where am I going?

What is the purpose and meaning of life?

What are my highest values in life?

Do I believe that all people in the world are equal in dignity? Why?

Do I share the ideals of marriage mentioned in the first chapter of this book?

If not, what are my ideals of marriage?

Putting aside for the moment any creed I may have learned by heart as a child, and expressing things in my own words, what is my religious faith?

What do I really and truly believe concerning my relationship with God? with other people? with myself?

What answers is my partner giving to all the above questions?

How different are our values in life?

How different are the long-term goals we are seeking?

How different is our view of marriage?

Are there points where our different answers will cause conflicts?

Does either of us find the discussion of religion threatening?

Have we discussed the religious upbringing of our children? Are there potential conflicts on this point?

Are there any times when we discuss religion when the thing we ought to discuss is quite different?

Are there any times when we discuss something else when we ought to discuss religion?

Does my partner respect my conscience?

Do I respect my partner's conscience?

Has either of us ever tried to force the other to a particular way of thinking on a matter of conscience?

Do any of the teachings of my partner's Church cause problems for me?

Do any teachings of my Church cause problems for my partner?

Can we discuss such issues?

Do the discussions become heated?

Do we tend to avoid such issues?

6. Motives for Marriage

People usually marry for a mixture of motives, so it is dangerous to think that love is the sole motive. The mixture usually contains both the desire to do things for the partner and the desire to meet one's own needs. The meeting of one's own needs is usually more important to the individual, even when the couple are very much in love. It is the mixture that counts; that is, there is nothing wrong in seeking to meet one's own needs as long as the mixture is healthy. If, however, one or more of the following motives is the predominant part of the mixture, then it is not healthy:

- marrying solely because of a pregnancy;
- desiring to escape from an unhappy home situation;
- experiencing a sense of failure and a need for acceptance;
- having low self-esteem;
- being lonely and depressed;
- marrying out of pity rather than love;
- marrying solely out of physical attraction;
- being afraid of being left on the shelf;
- being "in love with love";
- rebounding from a broken romance;
- seeing marriage as a status symbol;
- seeking money or social standing;
- escaping pressure from a partner for a sexual relationship;
- feeling guilty about a sexual relationship;
- marrying after a long acquaintance because everyone expects it;

- being fed up with cooking and cleaning for one-self;
- marrying to "beat a girlfriend to the altar";
- feeling that marriage is "the next thing to do," the next "experience to try out."

The common factor in all these motives is that they are really negative reasons for marriage. Not one of them is the choice of another person as a person to spend one's life with for positive reasons. All of them involve some 'using' of the other person, a solving of some other problem through marriage.

 Some Questions for the Couple:

How many different motives can I find in myself for desiring this marriage?

In particular, what are the needs in myself that I am seeking to meet?

Is the partner I have chosen capable of meeting these needs?

What are my partner's motives?

What are the needs he or she is seeking to meet?

Am I capable of meeting them?

Are any of the dangerous motives listed above present?

How large a part of the mixture are they?

Am I in any way using my partner?

Is my partner in any way using me?

7. Expectations of Marriage

For most people their family life is the most important element in their satisfaction with life as a whole. It is there more than anywhere else that their needs are met or not met. At the same time, marriage is not the whole of life, it cannot fulfill all needs and it cannot solve all problems. If you expect it to, you could end up feeling that your partner has failed and cheated you. For example, if you have an unresolved problem in your relationship with a parent, or you do not know what work you wish to do, if you have problems of identity and self-esteem, or any one of a hundred other problems that are in no way directly part of your marriage relationship, then marriage in itself will probably not resolve the problem and may even magnify it. Your expectations are probably unrealistic if you look to marriage to resolve a problem in your life, but do not see clearly exactly how it will do this.

Some Questions for the Couple:

What are the unresolved problems in my life?

What are the unresolved problems in my partner's life?

What effect will marriage have on these problems?

If I hope it will solve them, can I see clearly exactly how it will do this?

What can I fairly ask of my partner in resolving my problems?

What can my partner fairly ask of me?

45

8. Communication

Communication requires a book in itself, but I must be brief. Good communication is one of the greatest assets of a marriage, but it is also one of the most difficult things to achieve and maintain. It is easy for a couple to think they have good communication when in fact they do not. It is not acquired automatically, but must be constantly worked at. It is easy enough at the level of external facts that pose no threat, but lack of communication always starts with matters that are threatening to either party. If a question is asked, one fears what the answer will be, so the question is not asked. Couples can be unaware that there is a communication problem. If the question is asked, people have all sorts of defence mechanisms for dealing with it. Most communication is non-verbal, so a sensitivity to feeling and mood is essential. At the same time, many people do need to have things spelled out for them, so whenever possible it is good to put feelings into words that convey a clear message. The most important communications concern feelings rather than ideas. The feelings that cause most damage when not communicated are fear, hurt and anger. For example, if something your partner has done makes you angry, it is no solution if you erupt in uncontrolled anger, nor is it a solution to bottle up the anger inside yourself. It is better to let your partner know, as calmly as you are able, that there are feelings of anger within you. If serious problems of communication arise in the marriage, it is important to seek help sooner rather than later. If your partner is convinced there is a problem of communication, then you have a problem too, whether you realize this or not.

? *Some Questions (among many) for the Couple:*

Do you feel at ease when you are with your partner?

Is your partner a good companion in doing things together?

Are there situations that make you feel uncomfortable?

Are you able to let your partner know that you feel uncomfortable?

What is your partner's reaction?

Are you ever afraid of your partner?

Does either of you have difficulties in putting feelings into words?

Can you both express fear, hurt and anger in an appropriate and constructive way?

Are you worried by a lack of sensitivity to mood and feeling?

Do even the most obvious things have to be spelled out in words?

Does one of you always have to be right?

If there has been an upset, does the first move towards reconciliation always have to come from the same person?

Are you a good listener?

Is your partner a good listener?

Does either of you talk too much?

What other defences do you both use, that is, means by which you hide your true feelings?

Does each of you express the appropriate feeling, e.g., if you feel fear, do you express fear or do you erupt in anger instead?

Are there questions you are afraid to ask your partner?

If outside help is suggested, would either of you give one of the two classic defence answers: "We can solve our own problems," or "I don't need help. If you do, go and get it."

9. Emotional Intimacy

Emotional intimacy is communication taken to a deeper level. It is one of the major goals of most people in getting married. When achieved, it brings a deep sense of unity and meets many needs. Many marriages, however, never achieve it to any great degree. In fact, inability to handle emotional intimacy is one of the major causes of marriage breakdown. The fear involved is a fear of the vulnerability to hurt, the defencelessness that comes from letting another person get too close to me and know too much about me. Defence mechanisms can work overtime to keep the other at a safe distance. Conflicts occur when one partner has a deep need for such intimacy and the other has a deep fear of it. Often, of course, both the need and the fear can exist within the one individual. At the same time there are limits to emotional intimacy. In marriage a couple become one, but they should not lose their individual identity as persons; no one has a right to know a partner's every last fantasy and secret fear, every single, even minor, event, of the past of which an individual feels ashamed. The more common defect, however, is that of insufficient intimacy. Intimacy is a gift, but marriage creates expectations and pressures in regard to it. If serious conflicts arise, competent help should be sought quickly. The secret of intimacy is trust. I will reveal my inner self only to someone I trust completely. If the revelation is then used against me, I will rapidly cease to make further revelations. Intimacy must be worked at: many marriages reach only a certain level and then stay there forever. Intimacy takes time to achieve; it does not come about as the result of one conversation, no matter how honest and frank it may be. It is a process of growing together.

Some Questions for the Couple:

> *What thoughts, feelings or events of my past life do I fear to reveal to my partner?*
>
> *Are there things my partner needs to know if we are to achieve a good degree of emotional intimacy?*
>
> *If I am reluctant to discuss these things, what is the basis of my fear—that my partner might leave me? or despise me? or use them against me? or is it a fear of getting too close?*
>
> *What defence mechanisms do we both use to keep the other at a safe distance?*
>
> *Do I feel that my partner keeps too much emotional distance between us? or wishes to get too close?*
>
> *Can we discuss this?*

Is there too much emotional distance because either of us is too rational—analyzing everything and feeling nothing?

Do I trust my partner enough to become vulnerable?

Does my partner trust me enough to become vulnerable?

Does either of us always like to have other people around so that we are not alone enough?

10. Finances and Home Management

There are practical skills to be learned in marriage as in any other field of activity. Failure to learn these skills can cause problems in all aspects of the marriage. At times seemingly small things can assume very great importance because of reactions they cause in the whole relationship. These practical skills include budgeting and the sensible use of money, a realistic assessment of housing prospects, proper maintenance of the home, insurance, cooking and cleaning, furnishing and decorating of a home and, in general, creating a secure family environment. Eventually they will include all aspects of child care.

Some Questions for the Couple:

How well are we both prepared in these practical matters?

If there are large gaps, what are we doing about them right now?

Are there any debts at present? Where did they come from?

Have we both saved some money?

If not, what is this saying about one or both of us?

Have we agreed on the material standard of living we wish to achieve?

Are our ideas on this point good for our marriage: e.g., would they mean that we had to defer children for longer than is good for our relationship?

How fixed are our ideas on this subject: e.g., would we be prepared to adapt if the unforeseen happened (an illness, a pregnancy)?

How realistic are our ideas: e.g., do we want the world, but would resent the work and absence from each other necessary to obtain it?

Do we want everything immediately, or are we prepared to go slowly?

What are our real priorities in this regard?

Have we agreed on who will be in charge of handling money, operating bank accounts, etc.?

11. In-laws

Marriage necessarily involves a relationship with the family of one's partner. If this goes well, it can enrich a person's life. If it goes badly, it can be a painful cross and can pose a real threat to the marriage.

? *Some Questions for the Couple:*

Do I have the feeling that I am being required to marry an entire family? that I will become a junior member of a tribe? that my partner will still take orders from parents? that decisions will be discussed with parents but not with me? that any decision we reach together could be overruled by parents? that any assistance they give us has strings attached?

On the other hand, do I wish to cut my partner off entirely from his or her family?

Would I resent even a genuine offer of help and brand it as interference?

Do I resent the closeness of the members of my partner's family because my own family did not have the same closeness?

Or, on the contrary, is my attraction more to the family life than to my partner, e.g., because my partner's mother is felt to be more of a mother to me than my own mother, am I seeking a mother rather than a husband or wife?

How do I get on with my partner's brothers, sisters and other relatives?

Is it important to me that we always live close to my parents?

Can I "leave father and mother and cling to my wife (husband) and the two become one body"?

What are the answers if the questions are now turned around to refer to my partner: e.g., does my partner have the feeling of being required to marry an entire family, etc.?

12. Sexuality

The sexual relationship is a very important part of a marriage, though it is far from being the only important thing. Often, but not always, it acts as a symptom, a barometer, of how the whole relationship is progressing. Because it so frequently reflects the whole relationship, if it is unsatisfactory, it is good to discover why; the answer will often have nothing to do with sex, at least directly. Having sexual intercourse does not solve all problems in a marriage; if the attempt is made to use it this way, it will at best camouflage a problem and may well make it worse because one partner will feel used. Technique is not to be ignored, but is nowhere near as important as the expression of love. Knowledge of a partner's sexual needs and responses is important because it helps the expression of love. It is not at all good if the only physical expressions of affection are those directly connected with intercourse. The degree of tenderness and sensitivity that characterizes the whole relationship will usually be reflected in the sexual relationship, but the reverse is not necessarily true; that is, a person can be tender in sex but not otherwise.

No one is an expert the very first time he or she walks onto a tennis court; the art of lovemaking also has to be learned, so no one should feel a failure if there are initial difficulties. The marriage is not a failure if one spouse does not reach orgasm on every single occasion, but if it never or rarely happens, it is important to try to understand why. Everyone has certain fears concerning sexuality; it is far more healthy to admit this and face them than it is to bury them. For both men and women, our society places too much emphasis on sexual prowess and technique and not enough on other qualities that make a person a true man or woman. There is a psychological as well as spiritual truth to the idea of the couple becoming "one body": a physical familiarity with the other should grow to the point where all embarrassment disappears. Part of this is to overcome all embarrassment concerning one's own body in the presence of the other.

? *Some Questions for the Couple:*

Have I grown up with good feelings about sex?

Has my partner grown up with good feelings about sex?

What negatives were there for either of us in our upbringing?

What fears does each of us have?

Can we talk about these matters and express our fears?

Does either of us feel very uncomfortable in such discussions and try to avoid them?

Do I fear that my partner will substitute technique for love? will not express affection apart from intercourse? gives too much importance to sex? gives too little importance to sex? is lacking in tenderness and sensitivity? has no knowledge of my sexual needs and responses and no desire to find out? is obsessed with sexual prowess? will in any way use me sexually? will use sex as a weapon in any disagreements we have? will try to solve all problems through sex?

Does my partner have any of these fears about me?

Do I fear my partner's sexual demands?

Does my partner fear mine?

Am I happy with the way we now show affection for each other?

Am I embarrassed by my own body and sexuality?

Are there serious gaps in our knowledge of sex?

If so, what are we doing about them?

What is the attitude of both of us to fidelity?

13. Children

For the vast majority of couples, children are an integral part of their plans for marriage. If they are not, the couple need to think very, very seriously about what they intend their marriage to be. Because children are an integral part for most couples, the matter may be taken for granted. This is dangerous, as the two individuals may have quite different ideas on a number of matters relating to children.

? *Some Questions for the Couple:*

Do we both wish to have children from the marriage?

Have we talked this through thoroughly, and are we both firmly agreed on this?

Do I have any doubts about whether my partner wishes to have children?

How does my partner act towards any children he or she meets?

Do we wish to defer having children and, if so, for how long?

Are there potentially dangerous disagreements between us on this point?

Are there serious conflicts between us on how many children each of us would desire?

Are there conflicts concerning the method of limiting the number of children?

Do I have fears that my partner would resent children because they would interfere with our own relationship?

Would I myself resent children for this reason?

Do I have fears as to whether my partner will accept the responsibilities of parenthood?

Am I myself afraid to accept the duties of a parent?

Have we discussed methods of childraising?

Are our ideas on this compatible?

Have we discussed the role of a father? of a mother?

Since all couples have some fears concerning children, can we talk about these fears?

14. Couples from Different Backgrounds

With increased mobility, people are more and more contemplating marriage with persons whose cultural, social, economic, religious and educational backgrounds are different from their own. The greater the difference between a couple, the greater will be the need to discuss matters such as their roles as husband and wife, their status in relation to each other, how decisions are to be made in the family, the place of in-laws in their relationship, the care of children, wives working outside the home, the control of finances, the choice of friends and individual freedom. Their different backgrounds can easily have conditioned them to different expectations in marriage in relation to topics such as these.

Happiness Is a Serious Business

There may seem to be many questions asked here, but marriage is made up of many different strands, and all should be considered. Every married couple can think of questions that have not been asked here but which have been very important in their own marriage.

The questions have not been designed simply to scare people away from marriage by showing its complexity. The questions were designed to show couples that there are many matters to be considered in getting married and that love demands that they be considered. If adjustment and change are necessary, then the best time for that is before marriage. Should the questions lead a couple to decide that they do not belong together in marriage, then the best time to decide that is before they make a final commitment.

I also hope that the questions will help some married couples to achieve better communication and intimacy in their marriage. I would hope that no couple would use the questions to discover how unhappy they are unless they also use them to improve their relationship. Outside help is available, and can be of assistance in working through problems, if goodwill is present on both sides.

Preparing for marriage should be a most joyful period of a person's life. Anyone who tried to take the joy out of it would be destroying something good. Every real happiness, however, has an underlying seriousness to it; this is what makes it last. Preparing for marriage is a joyful time, but there is a lot of serious work to be done during it. If a couple wish to aim for the highest joy of "regaining the creation," then the work will be fully worthwhile.

Chapter Three

External Forces in Marriage Breakdown

$\mathscr{T}$he last chapter attempted to identify factors that contribute to problems in marriage, and which come from within the marriage itself. This chapter will attempt to look at some of the deeper currents at work in Western society that may undermine marriage. What follows does not apply to cultures other than those of Western society; for those other cultures the forces at work have been quite different.

The Nuclear Family

In earlier times most people lived in villages and worked on the land. They worked long hours with primitive tools. Husband and wife worked together or at least contributed very directly to each other's work. Neither could cope without the other. They therefore usually stayed together, even if their marriage was not ideal.

Very frequently the couple and their children did not live alone. Grandparents, uncles and aunts, married brothers and sisters often lived under the one roof. This tended to keep couples together, both because of the social pressures it brought to bear and because of the escape valves it provided for tensions in the marriage. Social factors perpetuated this situation through centuries.

It would, of course, be quite false to give an idealized picture of the village family life of earlier centuries. Many people, the women especially, often suffered severe hardship and injustice within this system. It was usually a rigidly structured society and was often narrow and confining in the opportunities it offered to individuals. At the same time, with all its faults, it was a socially viable system. It gave a basis to society and cared for the essential needs of the four groups: the young, the married, the single and the elderly.

In Western society it was the Industrial Revolution that gradually changed this pattern of living. Factories and the commerce that went with them demanded a greater concentration of people and so the cities came into being. Larger family groupings began to disperse as young people moved to the cities. The nuclear family—father, mother and children living alone without other relatives—became the norm. This gave a freedom to couples they had often not had before. It was necessary for many of the good developments that have taken place in family life, such as the greater sense of equality of the partners and the greater opportunities for personal fulfillment. At the same time, city living also created problems for the same four groups of people:

• It created the problem of care of the elderly, a problem we have certainly not resolved.

• Single people, who were usually about one in ten of the adult population, could now be left out in the cold. This problem has also not been resolved.

• It created problems for children because the role of being a parent became more difficult. There were no longer any of the checks and balances that existed in the wider family. For example, if a father in the wider family was overly severe, there was often an uncle or grandparent present under the same roof to give an example of another way a man could act. In the nuclear family there was only the model of the father from which to learn. More was now demanded of parents, and their defects were magnified as far as their children were concerned.

• It created problems for the couple themselves. Work was away from home, and frustrations with a superior at work could be taken out on the wife and children. The wife's frustrations with the children could be taken out on the husband. In many cases, the need for the wife to work outside the home meant having to cope with a quite different pattern of family interaction. The couple's tensions with each other had no escape valves by the presence of other relatives. There were no grandparents to act as live-in babysitters to enable parents to escape problems for a while. All the problems of city living began to affect marriage. Thus couples were thrown back more and more on their own inner resources. Many of them became stronger and better for it, as they sought new forms of family life to replace the old, but inevitably a number of marriages began to break down under the pressures.

These were some of the more direct effects of the Industrial Revolution on marriage, but that Revolution was to have a far greater effect on marriage through the effect it had on individuals.

Alienation

Technology has solved some of the problems presented by the Industrial Revolution. But in doing so it created a new problem, which is no longer capable of solution in purely material terms. This problem has been called "alienation." This term is used to describe the results of the widening gap between our work and the control we have over it.

In the pre-Industrial-Revolution village a man worked with his own hands at a job he knew and felt competent in, and so had a sense of achievement and of controlling his destiny. In a small community he was known and knew his neighbours, and patterns of mutual support were developed. If he was sober and industrious, he would be respected. By contrast, in the city he found that the factories and commerce could not function unless they were planned to a degree that reduced an individual's status to that of a very small part of a whole process. There was little opportunity for creative thought and action on his part. His work received no individual appreciation. In the larger city he often felt that few people either knew, needed or respected him. Thus he felt "alienated" from the society in which he lived and worked, no longer part of it. It was too big for him to influence affairs as he could in a village, so he tended to lose interest in his environment, to blame the system for anything he felt was wrong, and to look to the government to provide solutions.

Two World Wars, the Great Depression, the growth of big government and the welfare state, jobs being taken over by machines, the threat of nuclear holocaust, decisions made thousands of miles away producing an instant effect on our life, the sheer overwhelming size of modern life—all these things have contributed to the malaise, for in all of them a person is further reduced to the status of a number, a passive recipient. Men and women have lost the feeling that they control their own destinies.

The Rebellion of the 1960s

People were bound to rebel against this feeling of helplessness. The Wars, the Depression and the Cold War of the 1950s kept things quiet for a while, but rebellion had to come. The 1960s was a time of great unrest, when people stood up and asserted their own individual dignity. This decade could be described as the attempt to reassert human dignity, to place the human person above the machine.

The movement exploded simultaneously in forces as diverse as the Second Vatican Council and the Beatles. In one way or another, everyone felt the surge and was affected by it. There was a universal feeling that drove individuals to assert, "I am a person, I matter, I am important, I have a real human dignity which must be respected. I am not just a number on a card, a cipher in a computer file."

The movement was a good and necessary one. There had been a loss of many individual freedoms, there was not enough room for creative initiative, and many groups suffered real injustices. The lives of some individuals had become a soulless routine that dehumanized. Civil Rights movements and liberation movements—notably women's liberation—restored a lot of human dignity. The excesses that were indulged in during the 1960s and 1970s should not blind us to the fact that the urge for change was a good one.

At the same time it was a tumultuous movement, and we should not be surprised if there were also some defects. In my personal view there were two major defects. The first was that the movement spent most of its enormous energy on the less important targets, because they were easier to attack. It is easier to attack governments, social order, Churches and parents; it is much more difficult to change the machines of poverty, war, ignorance, "efficiency" and "economic progress," though these are the more serious causes of alienation. In many matters machines are undeniably more efficient than people, and one can wave any number of placards at a machine without influencing it in any way.

Thus many of the dehumanizing effects of the Industrial Revolution are still with us. Most recently, the spread of computer technology, with jobs it has taken over, shows us that the problems still remain to be solved.

In this conflict and with the weakening of many of the older values, it has been difficult for many people to find a basis for the assertion of their own dignity. They have suffered an identity crisis, a search for the basis of their own worth. The movement created strong enthusiasms, but it promised more than it could deliver.

There is a real sense in which the structures damaged in the movement—government, social order, Church and parents—are the very things most needed to overcome the more serious causes of alienation.

The second major defect was that the movement caused a considerable loss of the sense of community, of our need for each other. It over-emphasized the primacy of the individual, so that people began to ask, "What is good for me?" rather than "What is good for everyone?" The "Me Generation" included some who ceased to have consideration for anyone except themselves.

Very few people are strong enough to stand completely alone, to assert their own identity and dignity without reference to anyone else. For almost all people, acceptance by others is essential to their feeling of self-worth. Hence, while there has been the cult of the individual, of being oneself, there has also been, at times, the contrary force of a desperate search for acceptance and love from others and thus of conformity to a peer group.

Much attention has been given to the effects of alienation on the young and their rebellion against it. Admittedly, the young are more vulnerable, since part of growing up in any age is the search for a personal identity distinct from that of parents. However, the same forces are also present for the not-so-young. Adults who feel alienated may abuse addictive drugs such as alcohol and codeine, and the rebellion and search for meaning may merely be postponed to middle age.

Effects on Marriage

How people handle the situation created by the forces just described will depend on the particular mixture of circumstances and personality that makes up the life of each individual. Tensions are not necessarily destructive; they can equally be creative. There is ample evidence of people who have become stronger and better because of such tensions. At the same time it is not difficult to see how these forces have contributed to a higher rate of breakdown of marriage.

The sense of alienation has meant that more is expected of marriage today than in the past. Expectation of what it can do for an individual are often quite unrealistic. Some young people believe that through marriage the happiness of the present moment will automatically last forever. They have a confused hope that marriage will somehow resolve all problems of acceptance, self-image, identity, and living in an industrial society. Such couples feel cheated or deceived when marriage leaves unresolved problems in their lives.

For most people, satisfaction with home life is still the most important element of satisfaction with life as a whole. Home life is the primary source of support, encouragement and sympathy. Dissatisfaction with the problems that marriage leaves unresolved leads to criticism, and criticism by a spouse hurts because it affects one's own value of oneself far more deeply than would any outside criticism. It leads to a self-protective counterattack. In an age when self-image is both so important and so brittle, the attack on a person's sense of his or her own worth from one who is expected to give support can lead to a vicious circle, ending in breakdown.

Alienation has also meant that many people feel unable to plan an uncertain future, so they live by instinct and feeling rather than by a real knowledge of what to do. Ideas have often been confused, so feelings have predominated. Instinct and feelings, however, are concerned with the present moment, with how a person feels now, so we have seen a cult of the here and now. This has led to an emphasis on escapism, on material goods, on the romantic, on satisfaction here and now. These feelings can create problems in marriage because marriage is essentially a commitment into the long-term future. Marriage is not based solely on the fact that I like this person now, that this person fulfills my needs of the present moment; it is based on the commitment to build my future life on my relationship with this person to whom I now make myself vulnerable. This needs a firmer basis than a feeling concerning the present moment.

Most important of all in explaining the effects of alienation on marriage is the fact that, as demands on the marriage and on each other mount, a greater number of people simply cannot cope with them. The most common cause is an inability to cope with emotional life—one's own and that of the other members of the family. A person may be highly successful in other areas of life, but the demands of a close personal relationship can be too much. Everything possible is then done to escape from these emotional demands. Communication is the first casualty; absence is the most common form of escape; and physical violence is often the last means of such escape. Marriages break down far more often because of this inability to cope than they do for malicious reasons.

On the other hand, the rebellion against the feeling of helplessness caused by alienation has sometimes meant that the demand for self-fulfillment by an individual can be destructive of the need to work together in a marriage. Marriage can be seen, consciously or unconsciously, as part of one's own self-fulfillment rather than a giving of oneself to another. Then the other is not being loved for himself or herself, but is being used for one's own self-fulfillment. Eventually, the marriage may be perceived as an obstacle to self-fulfillment. The increased acceptability of divorce has meant that a number of people are now less tolerant of frustration or restriction, and are less willing to compromise what they see as their personal interests in order to adapt to their marriage.

The same rebellion has caused many people to reject the Christian ideal of marriage. Even many Christians are simply unaware of such ideals. Often a couple, even though not openly asking the questions, are in fact giving radically different answers to such questions as: Who am I? Where do I come from? Where am I going? What is the purpose and meaning of life? What are the highest values in life? If partners in marriage are giving radically different answers to questions such as these, it will not be easy for their relationship to go beyond a certain depth. Yet the questions frequently remain unasked, either when choosing a partner for marriage or during a marriage. In the search for identity, the Christian would answer that every person has dignity because all have been created and redeemed by God, and that all are equal because all are children of the same Father and, therefore, brothers and sisters to each other. If the basis of identity, self-worth and the equality in dignity of all persons is not to be found in these Christian ideas, then where is it to be found? Other persons assert the dignity of each individual, but find it hard to give any real basis for the assertion.

Our Need for Each Other

Despite these trends, marriage will never disappear or even be seriously threatened with extinction. It is far too fundamental a relationship for that ever to happen. But the problems of an industrial society have not been resolved, so the same powerful forces are at work and marriage will continue to have its difficulties.

It would be tragic if the assertion of the dignity of each individual were to be lost or weakened; it is to be hoped that it will be balanced in the future by a new assertion of people's need for each other, despite the restrictions that this brings. It is only by helping each other that we can overcome the sense of alienation.

If I lived alone on a desert island, I could claim to be entirely free. There would be no one there to tell me what to do. I would be completely free to do whatever I wanted to do. However, I would not be as free as I might think. I would not be free to turn on the television or drive a car, because these things would not exist on the island. More importantly, I would not be free to meet other people, and I would miss out on everything that the presence of other people can give me. If I wanted the fulfillment that can only come through other people, then I would have to leave my island and live where others live. The moment I did this I would come up against their equal freedom and rights. Thus I would have to stop at traffic lights so that others could pass, and so on.

It is not traffic laws that restrict my freedom of movement; it is the presence of so many other people with their equal right to freedom of movement. If we did away with all traffic laws, we would not be more free to move around: we would be less free, and it would be dangerous to move at all. Good law does not take away freedom; it gives the greatest freedom possible in the presence of so many other people and their equal rights.

If I could not stand these restrictions, then I would have to go back to the desert island and once again have no people to meet. For almost everyone, the self-fulfillment that can come only through meeting people is more important than individual freedom, so we live within a community, with both the advantages and the restrictions that this brings.

Most people then seek that particular fulfillment that can be found only in the special relationship between a man and a woman that is marriage. Like any other meeting with people, it brings both advantages and restrictions, freedoms and responsibilities. Self-fulfillment then comes, not through each following some individual path to personal self-fulfillment, but through the relationship, with all its responsibilities and sacrifices of personal interest. It is here that a Christian ideal of marriage can greatly assist a couple.

No one can enter marriage today with any absolute guarantee that the marriage will last forever. For this very reason many marriages have been better and stronger. Since marriage cannot be taken for granted, many marriages show a greater degree of support, caring and sharing. If marriage is more difficult, it can be more rewarding.

Chapter Four

Learning to Live Again
After a Marriage Breakdown

$\mathcal{F}$ew people go through the breakdown of a marriage without some form of trauma. No matter how necessary the separation is, at the time it takes place, it is still the final moment in a human drama. The marriage had once represented an ideal, a dream of happiness, an investment of emotional energy and hard work in something most important in the couple's lives. This explains why people whose marriage breaks down are particularly vulnerable to self-doubt, depressions and a sense of emptiness.

There are many similarities between separation and death. Both are the loss of husband or wife. In separation the feelings can at times be more acute, precisely because the other person is still alive. While the person whose spouse has died may be able to find some comfort in the fact that death is inevitable, or in his or her faith in an afterlife, the separated person is given no such comfort.

Bereavement

Separated people frequently go through the same stages of bereavement as do people whose spouse has died. If the separation comes suddenly, without the slightest warning, the reactions will be very similar.

Diffent writers have expressed the stages of bereavement in different ways, mbut the following is not untypical.

There is the stage of *shock,* when a person has the cold realization that a marriage is heading towards separation. It can lead to a sense of numbness where people walk around in a daze, unable to think clearly.

A second stage is that of *denial,* the feeling that "this cannot be happening to me; other people separate, but it can't happen to me." It is a clinging to the original dream, a refusal to accept that the dream has gone.

A third stage is that of *guilt,* the feeling that something could have been done to save the marriage, a self-doubt, a sense of failure, a feeling of emptiness. This is obviously something that will eventually have to be worked through; it cannot be allowed to fester forever and destroy a person's life. However, such feelings are natural and should be accepted as natural. It is a danger sign if a person experiences no such feelings at all, because it can mean that they are being repressed and are therefore very strong, more than the person can cope with.

A fourth stage is that of the release of *grief.* Many emotions have been involved, and they must be released. This is necessary for a cleansing, a healing of the person as the grief is shared. Both anger and depression will be experienced, and there will be weeping and a feeling of disorientation. Memories of the past will be everywhere and will continually be evoked.

Needless to say, these stages will not occur in a neat sequence with clear gaps between them. They overlap and intertwine, and a person can temporarily move backwards. The process takes its own time, and there is not a great deal that can be done to hasten it. Knowledge of the process does not necessarily make it go more quickly.

It cannot be pre-planned, with a set time allowed for each stage. A most necessary virtue is that of patience with self.

Other persons can be most helpful by their presence and support, but they must not quickly tell the person to "snap out of it," because grief is normal and in fact necessary for the acceptance of loss. Most experts would claim that the process usually takes between two and five years and that even then it frequently leaves scars. While it would be harmful to continue to wallow forever in self-pity, it is far more common among English-speaking peoples not to allow sufficient time or forms of expression for grief, and this can be equally harmful. A person who thinks that the process has been worked through can suddenly be annoyed with himself or herself for bursting into tears again after a period of calm. It bears repeating that patience with self is a most necessary virtue in this situation.

Learning to Live Again

The final stage of bereavement is that of *learning to live again*. It is here that the separated person faces special difficulties.

There are the obvious problems of finding accommodation and of finance. Many people have to receive social assistance and welfare payments, which can be a hard thing to accept: a confirmation of their new status. It can mean moving to a new area, breaking the circle of friendships that has been formed. This makes recently separated people feel like strangers at a time when friendships are most necessary. Their grief is the loss not just of one relationship, but of many.

Most separations will eventually be formalized by a divorce, even if one partner does not want this. One

73

problem associated with divorce today is that it is obtained so easily. In many cases the court hearing lasts less than two minutes and the person can find himself or herself out on the street again and wondering, "Is that all there is to it? Are the years of my marriage legally dissolved so easily? Am I so easily turned into a divorced person?"

While most divorces are now a simple legal process, the same is not true of questions of custody, access, maintenance and property settlements. The well-to-do can afford to go to court, and some of the poor are provided for through legal aid, but most people are in between. Many have to settle for less out of court because they are unable to defend their rights in court or are financially unable to wait until the case is heard.

Then there are all the problems of acceptance by other people. This has often been described as the *stigma* of divorce. Although there is less ostracism of divorced people than in former years, there are still some people who hold that "good people don't get divorced," "if they had worked harder at their marriage, it would have worked," and "they should have prayed more." This critical attitude is particularly painful for a person who has not wanted a divorce, but who felt powerless to prevent the breakdown of the marriage. The stigma can also be extended to people who are separated but not divorced.

Separated or divorced persons need to remember that the most harmful judgments are the ones they make themselves, because these will go deeper. Often they will imagine that everyone else is judging them just as harshly, when in fact this is rarely the case. The separated or divorced person also needs to remember that often what may appear to be rejection by others is in fact a social problem that they share with others, with the widow and widower, the single mother and unmarried persons over thirty.

We live in a couple-oriented society. The number of single people in our society dwindled some time ago. In fact, the pressure to have a partner has in itself been the origin of some divorces, for people who knew marriage was not for them nevertheless married because they did not want to be thought strange or defective.

Since the social custom is to have a partner, a person without one can feel rejected. Most people over thirty move in a circle of married friends. Their friendships are formed through their children and with couples that both partners find congenial. Single persons—whether unmarried, separated, divorced or widowed—do not fit in, can be seen as a danger to the stability of the circle, and are thus excluded. Often single persons are not, for example, on the list to be invited to parties, or will be dropped from the list after losing their partner.

The marrieds are not necessarily being malicious or nasty to their erstwhile friends. They simply feel more comfortable in a group of couples. Many separated or divorced persons admit they acted in the same way when they were married. All the same, being excluded leaves the person without a partner feeling rejected.

There are more than enough hurtful remarks made that reinforce this feeling of rejection. Married people can feel threatened by the rising divorce rate, and so tend to look for oversimple explanations for the failure of other marriages. Thus their hurtful remarks are really defensive of their own positions. Furthermore, outsiders rarely know the full story, and moral judgments are out of place unless the outsider truly knows the causes of the breakdown. When moral judgment and rejection come from people such as parents or priests, it is twice as hurtful, because the separated or divorced person has a right to expect support from such people.

This sense of rejection comes at a time when separated persons are most in need of acceptance, a time of grappling with the problems of their identity and self-esteem, coming to terms with a broken marriage and seeking to redirect their lives. The greatest need can be simply for someone to whom they can really talk, so that they do not have to face all their problems alone.

It is small wonder that, as their numbers have increased, separated persons have begun to come together to give and receive mutual help. Groups that cater to single parents have flourished. One good thing that has come out of such groups is the simple feeling of acceptance, of not being alone. Often, for the first time, separated people discover that they are not the only ones facing a particular problem. They can receive help and advice from people who have been along the same path.

While groups such as these have met a real need, they are no substitute for acceptance in the wider community. For Catholics this means, in particular, acceptance in the parish where they live. Many separated or divorced Catholics discover, sometimes to their own surprise, that acceptance by the parish community is very important to them.

Sadly, many separated or divorced people feel that they do not receive this acceptance. There can be many factors involved. The persons concerned can sometimes be seeking the solution to all problems, and this is more than the parish can offer. Sometimes it is their own fears of what other people are thinking that get in the way. Sometimes a parish is geared to meet ordinary needs, but not special ones. Sometimes there are simply too many other special needs. Sometimes, as with widows and widowers, people are willing to rally around at the beginning, but do not know how to cope with emotional distress on a longer-term basis. Sometimes they fear a long-term, time-consuming involvement in the divorced person's problems. Sometimes it is simply that the bereavement process cannot be hurried. Sometimes it is a fear on the part of the priest or married couples that too much acceptance of such persons is dangerous to marriage. Sometimes it is a fear that the divorced person will remarry and force confrontation with Church teaching. Sometimes (it must freely be admitted) it is a judgmental attitude on the part of priest or people, though I would add that separated or divorced persons, for their own sake, should not immediately assume that this is so. Whatever the reasons, the question of acceptance is one that parishes must face, for the problem exists and will not go away. Separated and divorced persons have a deep need for this acceptance.

Another problem of separated or divorced persons is that of learning to trust again. This is a delicate and vitally important area. They have been hurt and do not wish to be hurt that badly again. It was said in the first chapter that to trust and to love is to make oneself vulnerable, and separated or divorced persons often fear becoming vulnerable again. Like any hurt animal, there is the temptation to crawl into a hole. It is not just a matter of falling in love again, but of trusting anyone again, especially a person of the other sex. It is a vitally important area, because it affects the whole of a person's future. Trusted friends can do a great service just by being there. Those who treat divorced people as "easy game" can cause deep harm.

Children

So far, mention has been made only of the personal problems of the separated or divorced. But there are also difficulties with the children of the marriage. The children may already have been hurt by the conflict that led to the separation. Now the separation and divorce have to be explained to them.

Often children of separated or divorced parents have to move to a new school and make new friends. They find it difficult to explain the situation and can be ridiculed by other children. Teachers can, in all innocence, put them in emotionally disturbing situations, e.g., by speaking and acting on the assumption that all children in their class have two parents at home. A teacher can fail to understand the cause of a behavioural problem that has arisen from a child's feeling of rejection or insecurity.

Often the parent looking after the children has to go out to work, and so has less time with them. Access arrangements can be confusing to children, since they sometimes place one parent in the role of provider and disciplinarian, while the other is in the role of a giver of presents and special treats. Children can be used in a battle between the parents. They can feel abandoned by a loved parent, or have to come to terms with a parent they dislike.

There can be deterioration in schoolwork because of the child's anxiety. There can be guilt feelings for "causing" the separation. There is sometimes an urge to punish the parents for separating by refusing to "perform." A child can even think that by creating problems he or she will force the parents to reconcile.

There are special problems with children who are adolescents at the time of the break-up. It can appear to the teenager as a close-up picture of adult failure. The inner conflict caused by the separation may bring about a break in the process of maturation and identity, leaving the young person with severe doubts about his or her ability to achieve meaningful relationships.

One or both parents can quickly become fallen idols. They now appear as inadequate and ineffective role models. A boy learns his model of how to be a husband from his father, a girl learns her model from her mother. Despite all the other influences on children today, their parents still remain the most formative influence in their lives. Outsiders may be admired and imitated for particular qualities, but it is the parents from whom all the details of day-to-day living are learned. The adolescent thus faces a confusion of models.

Learning Through Separation and Divorce

So far this has been a totally negative presentation, giving only the problems. This has been necessary because the whole community needs to be aware of the difficulties that separated or divorced persons have to face. A community awareness is necessary if problems are to be overcome. The number of separated or divorced persons today means that it is a large-scale social problem, which cannot be brushed aside.

The idea being propounded by some that divorce is no more than a growth experience, a stage of development, something that everyone almost ought to go through if they wish to be mature, is a sad caricature of the reality. Divorce hurts—it hurts deeply and for a long time. The only people who appear to escape from marriage with no hurt are those who have put nothing into the marriage in the first place, but I hope that no one envies them.

At the same time, the picture is by no means always as bleak as presented here. Not all separated or divorced persons experience the same practical problems. Not all of them experience the same rejection. There can be growth through a marriage breakdown, just as there can through any painful experience. Though it is not an easy process, valuable self-knowledge can be gained. For the Christian, it can be a true experience of death and resurrection. Marriage is not the only method of finding God. The Cross is the basic Christian method, and separation is often close to Calvary. As one divorced person put it, "Although I would never have had the courage to choose the path my life has taken so far, I cannot now say that I would wish to give up any of the insights so painfully gained in the (often most unwilling) process." Many have given to their children an example of selfless love that any child would envy and that makes up for any defects in the child's external circumstances.

Remarriage

In the following chapters I shall discuss the position of the Catholic in relation to remarriage.

However, in the context of this chapter it can simply be stated as fact that the majority of divorced persons do remarry. They see in this a solution to many of the problems they face, and they still seek the fulfillment of family life. However, contrary to popular belief, the percentage of breakdowns for second and further marriages is higher than it is for first marriages, so we must look at the particular problems involved.

Firstly, there is the question of motives. Chapter Two spoke of some dangerous motives that lead young people to marry early. Some of these are less likely to be present in a second marriage, but others can be present: low self-esteem; escape from the present situation; a sense of failure and a need for acceptance; loneliness and depression; a man fed up with cooking and cleaning for himself. If any of these is a major motive, then it is not choosing another person as a person to spend one's life with for positive reasons, and so is a dangerous motive for marriage.

Secondly, the same forces that caused the breakdown of a first marriage can, if left unchecked, cause the breakdown of a second. Something caused the breakdown of the first marriage; if the same forces are at work in the second one, they may have the same effect. For example, if a man's low self-esteem caused a compulsive need to assert himself, to the extent that this destroyed his marriage, then the failure of that marriage will hardly have helped his self-esteem, and so he may do the same thing in a second marriage.

Fault has been taken out of the legal divorce process, but people still think in terms of fault, especially in the period immediately after a breakdown. They can easily blame the other for the failure of the marriage, as this is a natural defence mechanism. Their only fault was to choose the wrong partner; if they now choose the right one, everything will go well. In some cases this is true, but it is a dangerous attitude. The cause of a marriage breakdown is only rarely 100 percent on one side. The lessons for oneself from a first marriage have to be learned. People shy away from this because it is a painful, and indeed threatening, process. Yet, if divorce is to be a growth experience, it is essential to learn from it. This cannot really be done until a person is ready, and is often best done with the assistance of a skilled person, but it is important that it be done before a new marriage is seriously contemplated.

People who have been divorced are among the first to say that young people should prepare seriously for marriage, but they may think that, because they have been through it once before, they themselves have no need to prepare. The higher rate of divorce for such marriages indicates that the opposite is true. At the very least, the new partner will be a different person and a whole new relationship has to be learned.

Thirdly, as mentioned earlier, there are similarities between separation and the death of a spouse. It can be just as dangerous for a divorced person to race into a new marriage as it can be for a widow or widower to do so, and for the same reasons. The bereavement process takes its own time and cannot be hurried. It varies from one person to the next. If people hurry into a new marriage while still in the middle of this process, they are inviting problems, especially if they are acting out of a sense of panic or from a feeling of inability to cope alone. Bereaved people need to have progressed a long way on the path to learning to live again before they are ready to remarry.

Chapter Five

As Long as We Both Shall Live

$\mathcal{I}$n the first chapter it was said that the nature of love and commitment demands that the marriage vows be for one's entire life and that, for the Christian, the love of Christ on the cross adds strength to this idea. In themselves, however, these are moral arguments to show that a person ought not to break up a union if this can possibly be avoided. They imply a moral guilt, greater or lesser according to the circumstances, when a person breaks up a marriage without doing everything possible to avoid the break-up.

These arguments do not tell us what should happen to a person when he or she is abandoned or, for the sake of the children and his or her own sanity, an individual has no choice but to leave a marriage. When a marriage breaks down despite a person's greatest efforts, how far can we press the nature of love and commitment and the example of Christ? Can such a person be free to marry again?

The Teaching of Jesus

To answer these questions a Christian will first of all turn to what Christ himself said. Indeed, for a Christian this will be the overwhelming criterion that cannot be ignored or set aside, for the Christian knows that it cannot be right to be selective with Christ's statements, accepting one because it is pleasant, but rejecting or ignoring another because it is difficult.

In chapter 19 of Matthew's gospel, Jesus was asked to take sides in a controversy between two groups of Jewish scholars. The school of Shammai held that divorce was lawful only on the grounds of adultery; the school of Hillel allowed it for much broader reasons. Because Jesus was such a kind person, the people may have assumed that he would agree with the Hillel. So he was asked, "Is it against the Law for a man to divorce his wife on any pretext whatever?" (19:3).

To their intense surprise Jesus did not agree with either school, but took a more radical position than both. "Have you not read that the creator from the beginning *made them male and female* and that he said: *This is why a man must leave father and mother, and cling to his wife, and the two become one body?* They are no longer two, therefore, but one body. So then, what God has united, man must not divide" (19:4-6).

As can be seen, Jesus was calling on God's original plan for marriage. When his hearers then quoted the law of Moses at him, he reaffirmed this: "It was because you were so unteachable that Moses allowed you to divorce your wives, but it was not like this from the beginning. Now I say this to you: the man who divorces his wife— I am not speaking of fornication[8]—and marries another, is guilty of adultery" (19:8-9).

This teaching was so new and radical that it shocked even Christ's closest followers. Their first startled response was: "If that is how things are between husband and wife, it is not advisable to marry" (19:10). The Catholic Church's first statement on divorce is, therefore, that any Christian view of it will be radical and shocking to contemporary wisdom. A teaching that became so bland and acceptable that it no longer shocked anyone would not be true to the teaching of Christ.

Marriage is a unique relationship made up of many strands. It is an *emotional* bond because it is based on love and on such shared experiences as the setting up of a home and the bearing and raising of children. It is a *physical* bond because it is based on sexual union and living together. It is a *moral* bond because it is based on the wedding vows. It is a *spiritual* bond because it has been blessed and sealed by God. It is a *legal* bond because it involves acceptance by the community of a couple's union and legal protection of their status. It is a *personal* bond, weaving these various strands together.

It is obvious that several of these strands can be broken. The emotional bond of love can cease, though the shared experiences can never be quite forgotten. The physical bond of sexual union and living together can cease to exist. The legal bond can be broken by divorce. In brief, the personal bond can seem to have ceased to exist as a human reality. This is certainly what contemporary wisdom would say.

However, in calling back to the creation, to God's original plan, Jesus is indicating that a marriage never disappears entirely. It is arguable whether the million tiny strands of love, shared experience, intimacy and ideals can ever really be sundered completely, but Jesus is rather pointing to the spiritual bond of a union blessed and sealed by God.

For the Catholic Church, a man and a woman are free either to make or not to make the agreement to marry, but if they make it, then God attaches certain consequences to their act. Something very profound happens, a bond is established that is no longer theirs to break as they will. A married couple can no more cease to be husband and wife than a brother and sister can cease to be brother and sister.

Marriage is a relationship resulting from a contract. When the relationship comes into being, the contract has done its work—it has produced the relationship of marriage. The couple are then bound, not just by the contract (which they made), but by the relationship (which God made to seal their vows). Their marriage cannot be broken, not just because they made vows of lifelong fidelity, but because it is marriage.

We can speak of separation at three different levels. Firstly, a couple separates physically, and then, in varying degrees, the human reality of marriage has been broken. Secondly, a divorce is obtained, changing the civil status of a person from married to divorced, with consequent legal effects. For the Catholic Church there is a third level, at which separation is impossible—the level of the bond or relationship sealed by God. Only the death of one partner can dissolve this relationship.

Beliefs and Laws

It is important to understand that we are here dealing with a Church belief, not just a Church law. A Church law can be changed by the Church, a belief cannot be changed. For example, there is a Church law that says that priests may not marry. Whether this law will ever be changed need not concern us here. The point is that it is a Church law, and no one disputes the fact that, if a Pope were ever to see a change as desirable, he would have the power to change the law. He, therefore, also has the power to dispense from the law for a particular case.

A Church belief, on the other hand, is seen as coming from God and so is beyond the power of the Pope either to change or to dispense from for any individual.

Thus, a Pope is not free to declare that Christ is not God, or that there are only two Persons in the Trinity, or that murder and theft are no longer wrong.

The Church belief in the bond of marriage could change only if the Church decided that it had misunderstood what Jesus had said and that his words had some different meaning. While much has been written concerning the words of Jesus on this subject, I would be guilty of grossly misleading readers if I left any impression that Church belief concerning the bond of marriage is likely to change in any significant way. All the evidence leads to the opposite conclusion, for the Church remains convinced that this is what Jesus said.

The Greater Good?

Why did Jesus say what he said? Is this the same Jesus who healed the sick and forgave sinners? The only reasons he gave were that it was part of God's original plan of creation in establishing marriage, that the couple become two in one flesh, that God joined them together and so no human can put them asunder.

Whether we can fully understand these statements or not does not take away from their authority. Christ's statements are not dependent on the reasons we can give for them. Our explanations may be inadequate or even false, but his statements remain.

We can at least ask a question: In a very difficult and emotional field, is indissolubility perhaps the best defence of the good of the greatest number of people?

On the one hand, not to be able to remarry creates near intolerable hardships, especially for a young person with children to care for. There would seem to be very strong reasons for saying that such people should be able to remarry. On the other hand, present divorce is creating problems for whole generations of people who are marrying now or who will marry in the future.

The fact of divorce creates its own climate and way of thinking. The door is always open: there is always the option of divorce. There is less incentive to prepare well, to enter marriage with the seriousness it requires, to work at it despite difficulties.

I am not suggesting that all divorced persons married carelessly, far less that they all left their marriages casually, but the cases are increasing where the seriousness of the commitment leaves much to be desired. The current divorce rates ought to shock and worry us; it is a pity that we take them for granted.

When marriages break down, there is always suffering and hardship. Where all are able freely to remarry, the climate of divorce is fostered and the suffering is passed to other people in greater numbers. It is becoming a vicious circle in which more and more people are hurt. Following Christ, the Church must take the long-term view of the greatest good of all people, even if it wins few friends in doing so. Did Christ perhaps make his statement because he knew that humankind would never come to such a difficult conclusion unaided? Our human tendency is always to help the person we can see and not to worry too much about the two we cannot see. Speaking personally, I know that I could never have come to such a conclusion without the aid of Christ.

I do not know the mind of Christ, for what I have just said is only a human argument and Christ's statement is in no way dependent on it. We must never forget that the seemingly harsh statement of the indissolubility of marriage came from the God of love, who cares for all his people of all times.

Guilt and Innocence

Could not Jesus have somehow allowed remarriage for those who were innocent, while refusing it to those who were guilty? Surely this would prevent casual divorce. The only answer I can give is that, the longer I work in marriage tribunals, the less I would like to try to determine guilt and innocence in marriage.

For example, a person who never experienced love as a child will not know how to love as an adult. A person taught as a child to gain things by manipulating people will often know no other way of dealing with others. A boy who hated his mother will often later seek to punish her in his wife. An alcoholic is punishing himself. The list is endless. Do we blame such people for their actions? I know that I would never want to enter this field of moral judgments, and I do not believe it was the way Jesus dealt with people.

Our civil laws did attempt something of this moral judgment by granting divorces on restricted grounds, such as adultery, cruelty and desertion. This often led to bitterness in divorce cases, as guilt had to be proved. It led to false, partial or one-sided presentations of the facts. Once civil divorce was introduced in 1857, there were always arguments for ending up with the one ground of irretrievable breakdown. The alternatives are really divorce for no one or divorce for anyone who wants it. It is impossible to hold a line somewhere between the two. The line would be artificial and the injustices it causes could be shown.

The reasons of Jesus for the indissolubility of marriage are obviously deeper than the ones I have just given. He does not speak of pragmatic reasons, but points to God's original plan and essence of what marriage is. I do not know whether what I have said was in any way part of his thinking. I know only that he said, "the man who divorces his wife and marries another...." I know that his words shocked his hearers and, as a follower of Christ, I know of no method of explaining them away. And I know that I would never accuse him of not caring about the suffering of people.

Separation, Divorce, Remarriage

I said earlier that there is a moral guilt in a person who breaks up a marriage without first doing everything possible to avoid this breakdown. On the other hand, no one can talk of moral guilt if a person is abandoned by a partner against his or her will, or if, for the sake of the children and his or her own sanity, there is no choice except to leave a marriage. Thus, whether separation is wrong or not depends on the circumstances of the particular case. The decision is one that the individual must make in conscience before God alone, and no one is entitled to judge it. The Church is well aware that often there is no alternative, that separation is a necessity.

The Church also realizes that a civil divorce can sometimes be necessary—for protection against a partner, for custody and maintenance arrangements, for property settlements, for the security the law can give, or simply in order to put the past behind one and learn to live again. In such cases there is, therefore, no moral guilt. Such a person is in no way cut off from the Catholic Church and may receive the sacraments as often as he or she wishes. The common idea that every divorced Catholic is automatically excommunicated is false.

It is the third element, remarriage, that the Church cannot allow. Neither partner can remarry because, despite the divorce, they remain husband and wife. Thus neither is free to remarry in the Catholic Church, nor can the Church recognize a remarriage that takes place elsewhere. However, this applies only when a true and unbreakable bond does in fact exist, and this is what we must now discuss.

Chapter Six

Weddings that Are Not Marriages

Every Wedding Is Public

$\mathcal{F}$or any community the family is the basic cell of all social living. Most of the really important things in life are learned in the family—things such as loving, caring, sharing. For this reason marriage is so important that the whole nation has a legitimate interest in it.

This is the reason why every wedding must take place publicly. No matter how small the group of persons present may be, the authorized celebrant and the two witnesses represent the entire community. Through them the couple are making their vows publicly before the whole world.

In its long history, marriage has always been caught between two forces—each individual's search for personal happiness on the one hand, and the needs of the whole community on the other. In earlier years the needs of society often predominated; today there has been a reaction against this. This greater insistence on personal happiness is a legitimate one, but at times it tends to push aside the needs of society. Some people reject the needs of society or at least see them as outside interference. For such couples marriage is entirely what they want it to be. This was summed up in the words of the song: "We'll build a world of our own which no one else can share."

Within this viewpoint there is even a certain logic in some couples deciding to live together rather than marry. If marriage is only "a piece of paper," if it means nothing in itself and has nothing to do with anyone else, then why get married? Yet many couples who begin by living together do end up getting married. There can be many reasons for this, but some at least are reaching out for something more—a sense of security and permanence, an acceptance by the whole community. Without going as far as accepting that marriage is sacred, some seek to borrow from that sacred idea of marriage.

No couple can really "build a world of their own," for their marriage will be lived in the midst of the community. They and the community will interact on each other. If I drive through one little red light, I might not see this as having any large effect on the whole community, yet our road fatalities are the result of thousands of people taking risks or being careless. If I drop a piece of paper on the ground, I might well ask what difference that small object will make, yet the tons of litter collected each day are the result of thousands of people doing the same thing.

I am part of society and what I do has its effect on others. One marriage more or less might not seem to have much effect on society, yet the total of all marriages is infinitely more important to the health of a nation than traffic laws or litter. It is for these reasons that every society has its laws concerning marriage. These laws treat who may marry, the form in which they must marry and something of the content and effects of the marriage they enter.

Couples are, of course, free to enter many different kinds of union. They are not, however, entitled to call all of them "marriage." They may use the word "marriage" only when their union meets the conditions and contains the elements that are demanded by the community. The first chapter dealt with the ideal of marriage. Because society must protect marriage, this chapter deals with its minimum content, the point below which we cannot even speak of marriage at all.

For the Christian community, marriage also has a certain God-given content. For Christians, there is always another witness to marriage: Christ himself. The Catholic Church believes that it can use the word "marriage" only when it is marriage as God created it, when it has at least the minimum of the content God gave it. If that minimum content is not there, then the union may be called by whatever name people wish to give it, but as for the Church it is not marriage.

Decrees of Nullity

Against this background we can now look at decrees of nullity. *Precisely because the Church holds so strongly to the indissolubility of marriage, it must face the question of who is married. Precisely because it believes that there is a content to marriage, it can sometimes declare that people who have been through a wedding ceremony are not married.*

This is the meaning of a decree of nullity. A decree of divorce says that a marriage was there, but is now dissolved. A decree of nullity is a declaration that despite appearances and their good faith, a couple have never really been married, and each of them is therefore now free to get married, unless a prohibition is attached to the sentence or decree of nullity.

The idea that two people can go through a wedding ceremony and still not be married is not a new one. In Christian tradition it goes right back to the New Testament. In John 4:17-18 Jesus said to the Samaritan woman at Jacob's well: "You are right to say, `I have no husband.'" In 1 Corinthians 5:1-8, St. Paul condemns the

Corinthians for accepting the union of a man with his father's wife. The practice of declaring certain unions invalid has been there ever since.

Every legal system has provisions for declaring marriages null. That civil courts make such declarations only rarely is due to the fact that divorce is much simpler and cheaper to obtain than a decree that a marriage is null and void.

Catholic Objections

A number of Catholics dislike the idea of decrees of nullity because they seem to weaken the idea of indissolubility. They are seen as "Catholic divorce."

I said earlier that divorce causes further divorce, that there is a divorce mentality, that it would be impossible to hold a line between no divorce and divorce for everyone. Could it not be said that decrees of nullity would cause further decrees, that there could be a nullity mentality, that it would be impossible to hold a line between nullity for no one and nullity for everyone?

This is a serious objection that cannot be ignored. However, a Church that believes in indissolubility *must* face the question of who is married. Not to do so would be a serious injustice.

Indissolubility involves very great hardships for people who have suffered the tragedy of the breakdown of the marriage. Before we dare to ask people to bear these hardships for the rest of their lives, we have to ask whether they were married, whether there was that irrevocable bond in the first place. To allow the hardships without asking the question could not be justified. Indissolubility applies only where there is a marriage.

Furthermore, indissolubility and the content of marriage go together. They are two aspects of the same reality.

If marriage has no content, then it cannot be indissoluble. To say otherwise would be to claim that a contract devoid of all content was nevertheless binding forever. If we defend the indissolubility of every marriage, no matter what its content, then we are denying that marriage has a content.

The pastoral work of the Church must be based on these twin values of indissolubility and the content of marriage. It is no solution to the practical problems that arise if we say that it is all indissoluble, no matter what it is.

The analogy with the divorce mentality is not accurate. It is impossible to foresee a day when a decree of nullity would be as automatic as a divorce or as simple to obtain. The Church makes a very rigid distinction between the minimum content of a marriage and the perfect ideal of marriage.

I do not believe that the Church is ever going to lose sight of this distinction and raise the minimum content to the point where it covered almost every marriage. A person who married in the expectation of a decree of nullity if the marriage failed could be sadly disillusioned. Furthermore, it is possible to hold a line between no decrees of nullity and decrees for everyone precisely because tribunals do not make moral judgments; they are not in the business of deciding who was guilty and who was innocent. They seek the objective fact whether, according to the laws of the Church, the marriage was valid or invalid.

Church Laws on Marriage

Thus the Church also has its laws concerning marriage just as the state has laws. The laws of the Church determine when the Church community can recognize a union as a marriage. The laws come under the three headings of impediments, form and consent.

Impediments are circumstances of a person or a couple that mean that they are not free to enter certain marriages. *Form* concerns the ceremonies of the wedding. Since it is the vows or consent of a couple that bring a marriage into being, defects in this *consent* can make a marriage invalid.

What follows is far from being a complete presentation. The warning must be given that in any legal system it is always dangerous to read a brief account and then be one's own lawyer. The old adage that "a person who acts as his own lawyer has a fool for a client" is just as true in Church law as in any other legal system. If these matters concern any reader personally, then he or she should seek expert advice.

Impediments

1. Non-age

If either party is below the minimum legal age (16 years for a male and 14 years for a female) at the time of the wedding, then the marriage is invalid.

2. Impotence

A marriage is invalid if it is quite certain that either party will be unable to consummate the marriage. It must be quite certain. When a couple seeks to marry, the benefit of any doubt will be given to them, i.e., they will be allowed to marry unless the impotence is quite certain. It can be noted here that, even when there is no impotence, a marriage can under certain conditions be dissolved if the marriage has in fact never been consummated.

3. Previous bond

It has already been said that the Church cannot recognize the remarriage of a person during the lifetime of a former spouse, unless the former marriage has been declared null by ecclesiastical tribunal or dissolved by the authority of the Pope, according to certain conditions. Such a remarriage can, therefore, be declared invalid.

4. Disparity of cult

A marriage between a Catholic and an unbaptized person is invalid, unless the bishop dispenses from the impediment. A dispensation is almost always given, though the Church is not happy about the lack of unity on basic questions that will exist in the family.

5. Sacred orders

A deacon, a priest or a bishop cannot marry. If a priest, for example, attempts a marriage, it is invalid unless he has received a personal dispensation from the Pope. In getting ordained, a priest voluntarily gives up the right to marry.

6. Public vows

A religious brother or nun who has made a public vow of celibacy cannot marry unless dispensed from the impediment.

7. Abduction

If a woman is forcibly abducted or detained, no valid marriage can take place, even if she is willing to marry, until she is set free. No dispensation will ever be given from this impediment.

8. Crime

If a spouse is murdered to pave the way for a new marriage, then that new marriage is invalid. No dispensation will ever be given from this impediment.

9. Consanguinity

Marriages of very close blood relatives are invalid unless a dispensation is given. A dispensation would not be given for a brother to marry his sister.

10. Affinity

A person cannot marry a deceased partner's parent or child and no dispensation would be given.

11. De facto relatives

If a couple lives together, then neither of them may later marry the mother or daughter, father or son of the other person.

12. Adoption

A person may not marry an adopted son/daughter or brother/sister.

Form

This refers to the public form or ceremony of a wedding. It was said earlier that every marriage must take place before the community. So if a couple "married" without an authorized celebrant and two witnesses present, the marriage would be invalid.

By Church law, every Catholic is bound to marry before a Catholic minister—that is, bishop, priest or deacon—unless the bishop dispenses from this requirement. So if a Catholic married before a minister of another Church or a civil celebrant without a dispensation, the marriage would be invalid. The one exception is a marriage before a priest of an Orthodox Church (e.g., a Greek Orthodox priest).

Since this is a law of the Catholic Church, it applies only to Catholics. The Church recognizes the marriage of two persons who are not Catholics, whether they marry in their own Church or another church or in a civil ceremony. The only requirement is that there be a legitimate ceremony of marriage, i.e., a ceremony that the law of the country would recognize.

Consent

At a baptism it is the priest who baptizes a child; at an anointing it is the priest who confers the sacrament, and so on for the other sacraments. The one exception is marriage. At a wedding it is not the priest who marries the couple. The celebrant is present only as a witness. He is an official witness who must be present because he represents the entire community, but he is still only a witness. It is the consent of the couple, their marriage vows, that make the marriage. They marry each other with the celebrant as witness. Thus a serious defect in that consent can make the marriage invalid.

1. Force and fear

If a person is forced into a marriage by someone else, even a parent, against his or her will by means of serious threats, then the marriage is invalid.

2. Deceit

If a person conceals or lies about something concerning himself or herself that is so important that the truth would be bound to upset the whole relationship, then the marriage is invalid. For example, if a person knows that he or she is exclusively or predominantly homosexual, but hides this fact from an intended partner, then the marriage is invalid.

3. Intentions against marriage

(a) Fidelity. Marriage is a union between one man and one woman with a vow of fidelity. If, on the wedding day, a person has the intention of being unfaithful, to

such an extent that the partner is not even being given the right to expect fidelity, then the marriage is invalid.

(b) Permanence. Marriage is a permanent union. If, on the wedding day, a person intends only a trial marriage and has the clear intention of going his or her own way whenever desired, the marriage is invalid.

(c) Openness to children. It is up to a couple to decide how many children they will have, but some basic openness to new life is inherent in marriage. If, on the wedding day, either party is intending to deny to the other all right to have children or intends to be the sole judge of the matter, such that the other will have no say in it, the marriage is invalid. A marriage is not invalid because a couple is unable to have children, unless there is impotency antecedent to the marriage and it is permanent.

(d) Sharing of life. A union does not have to be idyllic or perfect before it can be called a marriage, but there is a basic minimum that is essential. There must be a point below which we cannot seriously speak of marriage. A marriage can be valid when a couple are not deeply in love, but it would be hard to speak of validity where one did not even have a basic respect for the other, was simply using the other without any interest in or concern for that other, was intending to treat the other merely as a slave or convenience, was excluding any sort of ideal, however modest, from the marriage and was determined to trample on the happiness of the other. If such had been the intentions of a person in giving consent on a wedding day, the marriage would be invalid.

4. Insanity

If a person is so mentally ill as to be quite incapable of the logical thought necessary to consent to marriage, the marriage is invalid.

5. Lack of canonical discretion

This is the first of the two major new developments that have taken place in this field in the last century. It came as a result of the better understanding of the workings of the human mind that has been gained by modern psychology. It is based on the fact that marriage is serious, with very real, lifelong responsibilities and obligations and that, as a result, there must be some minimum proportion between the consent given and the reality of what is being consented to. Every married couple will freely admit that there is always a gap, and in fact a large gap, between what they knew on their wedding day and the reality of what they were consenting to, but invalidity occurs only when this gap assumes gross proportions. It is because of this gap that every society establishes minimum ages for marriage, for the very young cannot possibly know what they are doing in something so serious. However, a similar gross gap can occur in some people who are not so young. Different things can go wrong in a person's background and upbringing to such an extent that he or she is quite incapable of making any realistic evaluation of the marriage that is being entered. Serious anxieties or obsessions, total absorption in one's own seemingly overwhelming problems—causes such as these can lead to what is called a lack of due discretion. The term can also apply when, owing to circumstances, a person is in such turmoil at the time of the wedding that he or she is not capable of any logical decision about getting married.

6. Incapacity

This is expressed more fully as "incapacity to fulfill and therefore to assume the essential obligations of marriage." It is the second major development of the last century. It refers to those people who are simply unfit subjects for marriage, who were never meant for marriage, who cannot possibly live that lifestyle, people of whom even their relatives and friends would say "He/she should never have married." It is based on the principle that no one can bind himself/herself to the impossible, no one can give another person a right to the impossible. It can also apply when in a particular marriage there is such a clash of deep-seated needs that the harder the couple try to build a marriage, the worse it will become.

"Immaturity" and "incompatibility" are not, as such, grounds for nullity. As they are used in our society in relation to marriage breakdown, both words are so vague as to be virtually meaningless.

*　*　*

All the explanations given above concerning impediments, form and consent apply solely to the moment of the exchange of consent at the wedding. If they only arise afterwards, they cannot make a marriage that is valid suddenly become invalid.

The warning is repeated that the above is a very brief summary, which leaves many gaps. On the basis of this summary alone it would be most unwise to decide that there is an easy case for nullity or, for that matter, to decide that there is definitely no case. Anyone personally concerned should seek expert advice.[9]

Chapter Seven

Approaching a Tribunal

*T*o deal with requests for decrees of nullity the Church has set up a system of tribunals throughout the world to give decisions in its name. A decree of nullity is a statement that a marriage was invalid from its beginning, that there was an invalidating defect in the contract and so it did not produce the relationship sealed by God. A person who received such a decree of nullity would, therefore, not be bound by the bond of a previous marriage.

The tribunal system is a judicial system because the rights of both parties are involved and because the decisions cannot be made lightly but must be based on evidence. Tribunals can perhaps best be explained by answering the questions most frequently asked about them.

Some of the grounds mentioned in the last chapter can be proved by means of documents alone. For example, to prove non-age it can be enough to present birth and marriage certificates; to prove a defect of form, it can be enough to present baptismal and marriage certificates. The following questions apply only to cases where the evidence of witnesses is required.

Questions Asked by Applicants

1. Isn't it threatening to be told that my marriage was invalid?

As mentioned in an earlier chapter, marriage is made up of many strands—emotional, physical, moral, spiritual, legal and personal. Invalidity refers only to the basic spiritual bond sealed by God. In a decree of nullity no one is implying that nothing existed, that there had never been any emotional, physical, moral or personal bonds, that the past is wiped away as though it had never existed. However, the aim of the tribunal is to lead a person to see whether or not something was so seriously lacking that the union could not be called a marriage in the true sense of the word. If, with the aid of the tribunal personnel, you yourself come to the realization that it could not truly be called a marriage, then you will no longer find the statement threatening.

2. Isn't it better to put the past behind me?

Only if you are incapable of facing it. If we face our own past, we are much better able to handle the future. If we do not face it, we can make the same mistakes again. Facing our past is not easy, but, when it is approached in the right spirit, many people have found it a most helpful experience. If you approach a tribunal with this attitude, then we can hope that you will go away pleased that you came and feeling more confident of the future.

3. Are decrees of nullity given more easily nowadays?

Not in the sense that tribunals simply give them away freely, for that is not in their power. They can give a decree of nullity only when the evidence shows that the marriage was in fact invalid on a ground accepted in Church law. Owing to the developments of the last century mentioned in the last chapter, declarations of nullity are more frequent than they were in former years. Only in this sense are they "easier."

4. What is the percentage of people who are successful in obtaining a decree of nullity?

There is good reason to believe that a number of people who know that they would have no hope at all of a decree of nullity do not make an approach and so do not appear in the statistics. Some of those who do make an approach are seeking only to placate a parent or a Catholic boyfriend or girlfriend and can tend to lose interest during the proceedings. For various reasons such as these, no accurate statistics can be given. Moreover, statistics say nothing at all about an individual's chances of success. Whether you are successful or not depends on what grounds you have, not on percentages.

5. When is the best time to apply for a decree of nullity?

If your marriage has broken up only recently, and you are still so much in the bereavement process that you have not come to terms with the fact that it has broken up, then it is too early for you to approach a tribunal. On the other hand, if you have left it so long that you would like to be able to remarry in the near future, then you have left it too long, and the sooner you apply, the better.

6. If I want a decree of nullity, what is the first step?

Simply phone the tribunal in your area or contact your pastor or bishop's office, and you will be advised as to whom you should see.

7. Who are the personnel of a tribunal?

At a tribunal there are judges, advocates, defenders of the bond and notaries.

8. What is the role of the judge?

There are usually three judges on each case. They are in charge of the case, and they control each of its stages. Either personally or through someone appointed by them, they take the evidence of each witness. They finally give the decision on each case.

9. What is an advocate?

The role of an advocate is to advise people. He or she has been trained to listen to your story, advise you on whether there appears to be some basis for a case and on what would be required to present it, and then assist you in presenting it. An advocate is not quite the same as a defence lawyer, so come with an open mind. You will find a person ready and willing to assist you in a Church tribunal.

10. Who is the defender of the bond?

As the name implies, his or her job is to defend the bond of marriage and so to take the side opposite to the advocate. The defender is not, however, required to do this at all costs by raising useless objections when it is clear that a marriage is invalid. His or her job is rather to ensure that the full truth is presented, that all sides of a story are heard.

11. What is a notary?

The notary is the person charged with making an accurate written record of all evidence.

12. Are there formal hearings as in a civil court?

No, there are not. You would be interviewed in an informal atmosphere. No one else would be present. A written record will be made of the interview. Each witness would then be interviewed in the same way, though not necessarily on the same day or in the same place. The decision will finally be made on the basis of the written record of all the testimony.

13. Will I be cross-examined?

No, there is nothing of this. The interview will be a friendly one carried out by only one person, whose aim is to help. Forget all ideas of courtroom scenes from television. Church tribunals bear no resemblance to such scenes.

14. What story would I be required to tell?

The important moment in a Church nullity case is the moment of the wedding. So the story will go back into family backgrounds, the courtship, the dynamics of the relationship, the story of the marriage and what has happened to each party since the separation. By having the whole picture, it is much easier to put the moment of the wedding into a context.

15. Will my former partner be contacted?

If the case is to go ahead, your partner must be contacted. The marriage involved two people and both have a right to know that a decree of nullity is being sought. This is a requirement of natural justice.

16. What if my partner refuses to cooperate?

Your partner will be contacted by the tribunal and invited to come in for an interview. If he or she refuses to cooperate or does not answer the letter, the case will go ahead without your partner.

17. What if I do not know where my former partner is now?

You would be obliged to make serious efforts to locate your partner, but if it is not possible the case would go ahead without him or her. In this situation the defender of the bond would have the task of seeing that your partner's rights are respected. The defender's first task would be to ensure that everything possible and reasonable had been done to locate your partner.

18. Will I have to confront my partner at the tribunal?

No, this is avoided. Your partner will be invited to come to the tribunal, but it will not be at the same time as yourself.

19. Is it better for my case if my former partner does go for an interview?

Yes, it is much better. To have the certainty necessary to give a decision, the tribunal must be sure that it has heard the full story. It is much easier for the tribunal to be certain if it has heard both parties.

20. Does this mean that the tribunal does not believe what I say?

No, it does not mean this. It means only that all of us see things through our own eyes. With the best will in the world, any one person will find it difficult to give the whole story of a relationship such as marriage.

21. Is the tribunal then trying to judge between me and my partner?

No, the tribunal is in no way involved in the field of moral judgments, in deciding who was right and who was wrong, who was to blame and who was innocent. A decree of nullity is not decided on the basis of dividing up blame for the breakdown of the marriage, but solely on the basis of whether one of the grounds of nullity mentioned in the last chapter is proved or not.

22. What happens if my former partner opposes a decree of nullity?

Your partner would have the same rights in opposing it as you have in presenting it. He or she could appoint an advocate, nominate witnesses, etc.

23. Can my former partner stop the case from being heard?

Sometimes people do attempt to do this, but it is the one right they do not have. If you have presented a case, no Church authority will stop it from being heard. If your partner wishes to oppose, this must be done by opposing within the system, that is, by giving evidence, naming witnesses, etc. In this your partner will be listened to as fully and carefully as yourself, and his or her rights will be fully respected, but the case will go ahead to a conclusion.

24. What if my partner has no interest at all in the tribunal decision, but merely wants to hurt me by preventing a decree of nullity?

The judges are bound to respect your partner's rights fully, but must also ensure that mere delaying tactics do not prevent a decision being given.

25. Will my former partner be informed of the grounds on which I have applied for a decree of nullity?

If your partner comes for an interview, he or she will be informed of the grounds of nullity and they will be explained.

26. How many witnesses will I need?

Two who know a lot are better than ten who don't. A few witnesses from both sides, or independent witnesses, are better than a long list of relatives of your own. Two perceptive witnesses are better than many who never saw beneath the surface. Professional witnesses, e.g., a psychiatrist, can at times do away with the need for others. The clearer the nullity, the smaller the number of witnesses required. All of this can be discussed with the person you see at the tribunal.

27. What if my witnesses live in another country?

They can still be named. The tribunal would then write to the tribunal in the place where the witnesses live and ask that tribunal to interview them.

28. What if I have no witnesses?

There are always witnesses. After listening to your story, the person you see at the tribunal will almost certainly be able to suggest several. A witness does not necessarily have to know the whole story. In many cases one will be able to tell us about certain things, another about certain other things.

29. Is it really necessary to bring other people into it like this?

Yes, it is. The rights of two people, the sanctity of marriage and the good of the community are all involved, so the tribunal has to be sure before it can make a decision that a marriage was invalid. Most people are willing to cooperate, particularly since they are not being asked to make moral judgments.

30. Who secures the cooperation of witnesses?

Normally you will be asked to do this, as they are much more likely to be cooperative if a personal request is made to them by yourself. A letter from a tribunal would not be nearly so effective in this. A tribunal has no power to coerce witnesses to appear, and in any case forced witnesses would be useless.

31. What do I tell my witnesses to say to the tribunal?

The truth. Nothing else will help. Attempts to make up a story would invariably be discovered. In fact, you will be asked not to discuss the case at all with your witnesses, so that they can give their own testimony objectively, just as they see it.

32. Is it necessary to obtain a civil divorce before applying for a decree of nullity?

A tribunal would not issue a decree of nullity with the consequent freedom to remarry until there had been a civil divorce. Normally the divorce would be obtained before the case is begun, as there can otherwise be complications. Normally a tribunal prefers that all civil matters (custody, property settlements, etc.) be resolved first, as otherwise conflicts from these cases can spill over into nullity cases, but it is realized that sometimes one cannot be sure that no such case will again arise, so the judges can decide that the case may go ahead.

33. Is the process a sort of Church investigation into the marriage?

No, it is a tribunal. If it were a Church investigation, then the tribunal would do all the work of seeking out witnesses, etc. But it is a tribunal, so for the most part it gives decisions on the evidence presented to it by the parties. So it is up to you, aided by your advocate, to seek witnesses, documents, etc. The tribunal will do what it can to assist you. The tribunal also has the power to demand evidence beyond that presented by the parties.

34. What documents am I required to present?

A full certificate of the marriage and a copy of the divorce decree. A Catholic is also required to present a certificate of baptism. In particular cases, certain other documents could be required, but you would be informed of this.

35. If I find it difficult to obtain documents or answer a query of the tribunal, what should I do?

It is always good if you know a priest in your local area who is willing to assist you by explaining a tribunal's request or helping you in finding a document or by generally giving you moral support in the process. It is strongly recommended that you have someone to assist and support you in this way.

36. If I have commenced a case, but do not know what is now happening in it, what should I do?

The tribunal could not cope if every one of its clients phoned up every week, but if you genuinely do not know what is happening, then phone and ask. You may be asked to phone back the next day so that your case can be properly assessed in the meantime.

37. How long does a process of nullity take?

The more important question is: What will the decision be? The answer to this question cannot be presumed. It would therefore be foolish for a person to rush the case and receive a "no" answer in a brief time rather than take the time necessary to present the case well.

38. Bearing this in mind, how long does the process take?

The time cases take varies greatly. It depends on how difficult a case is, whether witnesses cooperate, whether they have much to say, whether the other party opposes, whether there are any contradictions in the evidence, etc. Many delays are caused by the person presenting the case if he or she does not answer letters or changes address without informing the tribunal. The sheer number of cases being presented today is the major cause of delays. The person you meet at the tribunal will give you an idea of how long it may take, but will be unable to be definite because of all of the unknowns just mentioned.

39. What if my case is urgent?

Everyone's case is urgent, because all our clients are in the same position. If a tribunal took someone to the top of the list, this would be unfair to others, who have been waiting just as anxiously. In fairness to all, tribunals cannot work to other people's timetables. They can only do their best for everyone.

40. Will my case be stopped if I get married in the meantime in a civil ceremony?

No priest can give you permission to do this. If it is done, it is against the Church's teaching and is entirely your own responsibility before God alone. Once again it is presuming the tribunal's decision, and so could be creating serious spiritual problems for you. However, if you do this, the case will not be stopped, it will go ahead.

41. Can I bring a case if I have not been married before but wish to marry a person who has?

That person would have to bring the case.

42. What if that person is not a Catholic?

He or she could still bring the case, but would have to be cooperative.

43. Why would a non-Catholic have to present a case?

Because the Catholic Church would consider him or her to be a married person unless and until there was a decree of nullity of the earlier marriage. Only a Catholic is bound to marry in the Catholic Church, so the Church recognizes the marriage of two non-Catholics, even if they had been married only in a civil ceremony.

44. By what right can the Catholic Church make a judgment on a marriage between two non-Catholics?

The Church has the right to determine who may be married in the Catholic Church. It can make a judgment on the validity of a marriage of two non-Catholics because one of them asks it to, so that he or she may be able to marry a Catholic in the Catholic Church.

45. Does a decree of nullity mean that the children of the marriage are illegitimate?

No, it does not. A child is legitimate as long as the parents believed themselves to be married at the time the child was born, or even if they married after the birth of the child. As long as there has been a wedding ceremony and the couple were generally considered to be married at the time, there is no question of illegitimacy.

46. Since a decree of nullity means that a marriage was invalid from the beginning, doesn't it mean that a person would then have no obligations at all towards a former partner and any children of the marriage?

On the contrary. The union that existed created very real moral and legal obligations towards the partner and any children born. There could be serious moral guilt if these were ignored. This is the one way in which elements of judgment of moral guilt can enter the tribunal process. If a person seeks to remarry after a decree of nullity, the Church would insist on the fulfillment of obvious moral and legal obligations and would not allow a new marriage to take place in the Catholic Church unless they were being fulfilled up to that time. If there were doubts concerning the future, the Church would insist on a solemn written promise in this regard from both parties to the new marriage. This element of moral judgment has to enter in because otherwise the Church could become a party to the immoral ignoring of serious obligations by allowing a wedding to be celebrated in the Church while those obligations were being ignored.

47. Does a decree of nullity have any effects in civil law?

None whatsoever.

48. How much does a decree of nullity cost?

A tribunal has to employ staff, pay rent and generally run a large and busy office. Because of the common but false accusation that decrees of nullity can be bought, the Church is very sensitive about costs. No one is ever asked to pay the whole cost of a process. Every tribunal is subsidized from Church funds. In most tribunals two-thirds comes from the Church subsidy, only one-third from clients. From those who can afford it, a payment is asked. If a person cannot pay that amount, less is asked. If a person cannot pay anything, nothing is asked. No one is ever refused a decree of nullity because of an inability to pay. A rich person receives no priority, either in the time the case will take or in the way the case is handled. Costs vary with the type of case. You will be informed of costs when you contact a tribunal.

49. Why is it that the only cases we ever hear of are those of rich people?

Very few of the people who come to tribunals are either famous or rich. The cases of the majority are never heard of and create no publicity. The publicity focuses on the rare case of a well-known person, with the unjust conclusion that such a person can buy a decree of nullity, while other people cannot obtain them. If an occasional well-known person obtains a decree of nullity, this is because he or she is also a human being. The rights that all people possess cannot be denied to such a person.

50. Will my former partner be told what I have said and what the witnesses have said?

This is a tribunal's most serious dilemma. On the face of it, people have the right to know what is said about them, particularly if they wish to defend the case. To deny them this would be an injustice. On the other hand, tribunals rely entirely on the cooperation of people. They have no power to force witnesses to appear and answer questions. From experience they know very well that people will not speak to them if they think that what they say will be made known to others. So tribunals are forced to compromise. The witnesses are given a guarantee of confidentiality. The former partner is then invited to appoint an advocate. The advocates on both sides are entitled to see the written record of all evidence and to explain the contents of this evidence to their clients, but in such a way as to protect the confidentiality of each witness. Tribunals have to put up with the accusation of secrecy because the alternative would be to close down altogether, which would be an injustice to all clients.

51. I have heard that sometimes even the person who brings the case does not know why his or her marriage was declared invalid.

Every person presenting a case will at some stage be asked to sign a formal request to the tribunal asking for a decree of nullity. This formal request will clearly express the grounds of nullity and these will be explained to the person. It will then be signed personally by the person presenting the case. The other party will have the right to see this document. Tribunals are aware that some people then forget what they have said and what they have signed because they are interested only in the result. If they contacted the tribunal after the decree of nullity had been issued, it would be explained to them.

52. If my former partner obtains a decree of nullity and so can remarry, am I still bound?

No, it is the marriage that is declared invalid, so both parties are free to remarry. There can never be question of one being free while the other is still bound by the former marriage.

53. When the judges give their decision, is that final?

There is always a review of every decision by an Appeal Tribunal, which is directly responsible to the bishops of the country. In most cases, this review does not take long, but the decision is not final until it has been completed. A person opposed to a decree of nullity has a right of appeal to this tribunal. If the first tribunal's decision has been that it is not proved that the marriage was invalid, the person bringing the case has a right of appeal to this second tribunal for a new hearing of the case.

54. Isn't it true that every case has to go to Rome?

No, it isn't true, and never has been.

55. After a decree of nullity, is one always free to remarry?

Sometimes the tribunal will recommend professional assistance from, for example, a marriage counsellor, in preparing for a new marriage, so that problems that emerged in the first marriage can be avoided in the new marriage. Sometimes, where it appears that the new marriage would be just as invalid as the earlier one and for the same reasons, the tribunal may have to insist on certain precautions before a new marriage can take place in the Catholic Church.

56. When can I set the date for a new wedding?

No priest can accept a booking for a new wedding unless and until a decree of nullity is issued. To do so earlier is to presume the outcome of the case. Also the tribunal cannot work to your timetable, so it would create serious difficulties for you if the date you had set came close and no decree of nullity had been issued.

57. But if a tribunal has accepted my case and is hearing it, can't I presume that the answer will eventually be the answer that I want?

Emphatically, no. It is granted that, if you had no case whatsoever, a tribunal would tell you this at your very first interview or as soon as it became apparent. However, it not infrequently happens that in early interviews it is not certain whether there is a case or not, and then the tribunal will hear witnesses in order to clarify this. Even when it seems certain that there is the basis of a case, the tribunal does not know what the other party and witnesses are going to say or what complications and contradictions might arise. A tribunal can never guarantee the outcome of a case.

58. How do I answer people who object to decrees of nullity?

Almost everyone I have ever spoken to admits that some decrees of nullity are justified. For example, they would admit that a person forced into a marriage should be freed from that burden. Their objection is to any large number of decrees of nullity. Today, however, there are large numbers of people going through a divorce. Each one of them is an individual and has the right that his or her situation be considered. Any arbitrary limiting of numbers would be unjust. I have frequently seen people strongly opposed to decrees of nullity become instant and total converts when the marriage of their son or daughter breaks down. Everyone is someone's son or daughter; if one case deserves to be looked at, then so do all.

59. Isn't it an arbitrary system? How can any human being presume to decide when God has not sealed a union?

In so many matters God works through human beings. That is not nearly as efficient or certain as if God made known all decisions personally, but it is the way God has chosen. The Church is a community and like any community it is entitled to have its law concerning marriage. It is freely admitted that sometimes the decisions are very difficult and that there are many grey areas. The human decisions are fallible, but the individuals concerned can only do the best they can on the basis of the specialized training and experience they have received. The alternative would be to have no decrees of nullity at all, but this would be an injustice.

60. If a decree of nullity is so complicated, is it worth it?

It is certainly worthwhile having a talk with someone at the tribunal. This is much better than relying on hearsay or on other advisers whose knowledge might be inaccurate. At this stage you would not yet have committed yourself to anything. If a decree of nullity is possible, it can make your future life much more peaceful than it might otherwise be.

Stages of the Procedure

1. You speak to an advocate who advises you as to whether there appear to be grounds for a decree of nullity. If there appear to be such grounds, the advocate assists you in drawing up a statement, preparing a formal request, nominating witnesses and collecting the necessary documents.

2. The advocate presents this material to the tribunal.

3. A judge, a defender of the bond and a notary are appointed to hear the case.

4. Your former husband or wife is contacted by the tribunal and is asked whether he or she agrees with or opposes a decree of nullity on the grounds alleged in your formal request.

5. The evidence of the two parties to the marriage is taken separately.

6. The evidence of the witnesses nominated by the two parties is taken.

7. If necessary, any further evidence considered by the judge to be essential is also collected.

8. All evidence is made available in written form to the advocates and defender of the bond, who then inform the judge whether they are satisfied or wish further evidence. The judge decides whether further evidence is to be admitted.

9. The judge then declares that the evidence is complete.

10. The advocate and defender prepare written submissions arguing their respective sides of the case.

11. The judge gives a decision.

12. This decision is reviewed by the Tribunal of Appeal. If necessary, further evidence can be taken at this stage.[10]

Footnotes

1. *Familiaris Consortio*, Apostolic Exhortation of Pope John Paul II, November 22, 1981, ©1983 by Franciscan Herald Press, Chicago, Il., p. 9.

2. Loc. cit.

3. This interpretation of chapter two of Genesis owes much to Wilfrid J. Harrington, OP, *The Promise to Love*, London, Geoffrey Chapman, 1968. However, I have reworked the material and added to it, so I take full responsibility for what is written here. Harrington notes that the *ish-ishsha* etymology is popular only; it is not exact. He calls it a typical Hebrew word play. I agree with him that this is what the inspired writer intended, because it is the only interpretation that makes full sense of the passage. That the man can name the animals, but cannot name the woman, is at the heart of the story.

4. *Familiaris Consortio*, p. 9.

5. Much of the argument in this section has been taken from *Marriage and the Church's Task, The Report of the (Anglican) General Synod Marriage Commission*, London, Church Information Office Publishing, 1978, pp. 123-35.

6. Cf. Hosea, Jeremiah 2:1–4:4, Ezekiel 16 and 23, Isaiah 54:1-10. In a different tradition, cf. Song of Songs and Tobit.

7. Pope John Paul II, homily at Puebla, Mexico, January 28, 1979, *Acta Apostolicae Sedis*, vol. 71 (1979), p. 14.

8. This is the famous "exceptive clause" of Matthew's Gospel (cf. also Mt. 5:32). There are many interpretations of its meaning, but it certainly cannot mean that Jesus allowed remarriage after adultery, for this would make

nonsense out of the whole passage and the stand he had just taken. After just taking a more radical stand and shocking his hearers in doing so, he would now, in the same sentence, be going back on this and simply agreeing with the school of Shammai. On this basis we could not explain the reaction of the Pharisees (v. 7) and of his disciples (v. 10). The whole passage would be a contradiction. Among the many interpretations given, the most probable and consistent, it seems to me, is as follows: The Greek word used, *porneia*, does not mean adultery, but is a more general and vague word meaning "sexual uncleanness." This alone should warn us that the meaning of the phrase is to be sought in Jewish law and customs, not in twentieth-century problems. Many would say that it here has the same meaning as it does in Acts 15:29, where the Gentile converts are asked by the apostles to abstain from four things which, though not wrong in themselves, would be highly offensive to Christians with a Jewish background. As such, they are all of a temporary nature: Gentiles are to abstain from them for as long as they remain offensive to Jewish converts. They are to abstain from food sacrificed to idols, from blood, from the meat of strangled animals and from *porneia*. *Porneia* here certainly does not mean adultery, for adultery is forbidden to Christians in itself and permanently, not just on a temporary basis for as long as it is offensive to Jews. *Porneia* is here generally taken to mean marriage within the degrees of kinship forbidden by Jewish law. The phrase in Matthew's Gospel is then seen as an addition to the words of Jesus made by the early Church, indicating that the words of Jesus do not apply when it is a case of a marriage within the forbidden degrees of kinship. In such a case the couple should separate. Not all would agree with this interpretation, but I repeat that it is impossible to accept the interpretation that Jesus allowed remarriage after adultery without making nonsense out of his whole stand. It should be noted that a very similar saying of Jesus occurs in Mark's Gospel with no "exceptive clause" at all: "Back in the house the disciples questioned him again about this, and he said to them, `The man who divorces his wife and marries another is guilty of adultery against her. And if a woman divorces her husband and marries another, she is guilty of adultery too'" (Mark 10:11-12).

9. To anyone wishing to read more about this topic I recommend the book by Ralph Brown, *Marriage Annulment in the Catholic Church*, London, Kevin Mayhew Publishers, 1977. In some matters of a technical nature the book is already out of date, but it remains the best popular book on the subject in English.

10. For a full presentation of the procedure, see *The Code of Canon Law in English Translation*, Collins Liturgical Publications, 1983 or Publications Service, Canadian Conference of Catholic Bishops, Ottawa, 1983. However, canons 1671–1691, which deal with procedure in marriage cases, must be read together with canons 1404–1655, which deal with all cases of any type heard by Church tribunals. [Also helpful is *Canons and Commentaries on Marriage* by I. Gramunt, J. Hervada, and L. Wauck, Collegeville, Minnesota, The Liturgical Press, 1987; and *The Canon Law: Letter and Spirit*, pp. 571-659 and 811-949, The Liturgical Press, 1995.]

A G M V
MARQUIS
Québec, Canada
2000